The National Capital Writing Contest's 30th Anniversary Anthology

Poetry and Short Stories

PLUS
A List of Previous Years' Winners

Canadian Authors Association–National Capital Region
Crowe Creations
Edited by Sherrill Wark

Canadian Authors Association–National Capital Region
https://canadianauthors.org/nationalcapitalregion/

and

Crowe Creations
crowecreations.ca

Copyright © 2017 Canadian Authors Association–National Capital Region and individual authors.

All rights reserved. No part of this book may be reproduced or transmitted in any form or by any means, electronic or mechanical, including photocopying, recording, electronic transmission, or by any storage and retrieval system, without written permission from the authors except for the purposes of study or review.

Any resemblance to persons living or dead is purely coincidental.

First Canadian Authors Association–National Capital Region Edition May 2017
https://canadianauthors.org/nationalcapitalregion/

Cover photo from iStock
Interior Graphics by Catina Noble of Twig Works
Cover design © 2017 by Crowe Creations
Interior design © 2017 by Crowe Creations
Text set in Garamond; headings set in Gothic720 Lt BT

Canadian Authors Association–National Capital Region
ISBN: 978-0-9869031-1-3

CreateSpace
ISBN-13: 978-1545294307
ISBN-10: 1545294305

To all the poets and storytellers who illuminate our world and the readers who bask in the glow..

Acknowledgements

Matt Bin
Gill Foss
Sharyn Heagle
Sheila Martindale
Catina Noble
Anita Purcell
Arlene Smith
Carol A. Stephen
Sherrill Wark

Contents

President's Message	1
NCWC: 30 Years of Excellence	3
Poetry	
The Poetry Judge	11
1st, 2nd and 3rd Place	
Gunda	14
Anne from Toronto	16
Sunset	19
Honourary Mentions in Alphabetical Order	
A small grief	22
Relay	24
Too Long a Winter	26
Short Stories	
The Short-Story Judge	29
1st, 2nd and 3rd Place Short Stories	
The Flower Seller of Agra	32
California Pure	41
Extra Innings	49

Honourable Mentions in Alphabetical Order	
Unexpected	60
Night Swim	68
Distant Connections	74
Winners and Honourable Mentions of Previous Years	83
1992	84
1993	86
1994	87
1995	88
1996	89
1997	90
2005	91
2006	92
2007	97
2008	101
2009	109
2010	113
2011	122
2012	125
2013	130
2014	133
2015	137
2016	139
The Graphics Artist	143
The NCWC Coordinator/Anthology Designer	145

"It may be those who do most, dream most."
— Stephen Leacock

Canadian Authors Association–National Capital Region President's Message

by Arlene Smith

Entering a writing contest is an act of faith. Writers start with an idea, use words to build on it, and shape those words into living, breathing story or poem. With a vulnerability born in faith, they release the work of their hands, minds and souls into the world with the trust that they and their work will be respected and encouraged.

Through the National Capital Writing Contest (NCWC), our branch of the Canadian Authors Association has respected and encouraged storytellers and poets for 30 years. We have invited writers to set their imaginations free, to trust us with their valuable insights and ideas, and to brush fears and uncertainties aside so that they can grow as people and as writers. Writers share with us sacred memories, fearless predictions and funny incidents. Often their work leads readers to quiet epiphanies, or to look at an old thing in a novel new way and to re-evaluate a long-held belief.

Those who attend the annual NCWC awards night to hear the finalists read their entries know that the short stories cover every genre: mystery, humour, action adventure, mainstream literary, and romance. The poetry showcases the realm-busting artistry of our talented poetic creators. The variety and the creativity we see every year reassures us that storywriters, poets and creators of all sorts thrive in our ever-changing times.

We congratulate this year's finalists, and we are proud to respect and encourage them by showcasing their work here. May you enjoy the stories and poems that each writer shared with us in an act of faith. May they lead you to a quiet epiphany or an overdue re-evaluation of a long-held belief. May this work be a spark that sets your own imagination free.

Enjoy,
Arlene Smith, President, Canadian Authors Association–National Capital Region

Arlene Smith is a freelance writer and certified copy editor. She writes video scripts, speeches and promotional materials for corporations and government departments. She also enjoys writing fiction and has been published in *DESCANT* magazine and a *Writer's Digest* short story collection. When she's not writing, you can find her at the Ottawa Public Library where she works part time in her happy place — in the company of books.

National Capital Writing Contest: 30 Years of Excellence

by Gill Foss

In 1986, the Ottawa Branch of the Canadian Authors Association was already running a writing contest that served members writing poetry. The Branch Executive decided that the Association needed to expand its relevance locally with greater publicity in line with the aims of the National mandate: "Writers Helping Writers." The result was the creation of the National Capital Writing Contest (NCWC) open to all writers in the national capital region. The job of organizing this new initiative fell to the Branch President who just happened to be me, Gill Foss.

Previously with the original in-house contest, the branch covered all prize monies. This soon became a burden. With the extended scope of the new NCWC, this financial arrangement had to change. The decision was made to seek sponsors for a first, second and third prize in each category:

1. Structured poem: any traditionally accepted poetic form (sonnet, blank verse etc) up to 60 lines;
2. Short Free verse: any subject up to 60 lines;
3. Haiku: a set of three submitted as one entry; and
4. Short Story.

Although knowledge of what the entry fee was is now lost in antiquity, $5 per poem seems likely.

Inviting Prize Monies

The question then became how to find and approach appropriate sponsors and set prize amounts.

The first obvious choice was to approach the local daily — the *Ottawa Citizen* — well before its decision-making was moved to the Toronto office. We asked them to cover First Prize in each category in the amount of $100. This they agreed to provide as a cheque. We were on our way.

This left three second and third place prizes still needing financial support. We finally settled on asking some of the leading independent bookstores (most of which are unfortunately no longer with us) if they would be willing to step up and support us. Paul King of Food for Thought bookstore was the first to come on board followed by Propero, the Book Company, then Diane Walker of Shirley Leishman Books. These three sponsored Second Prize with either a $50 gift certificate or a coffee table book to that value. This left the last category. Peggy Harris of the Ottawa Women's

Bookstore and Joan Askwith of The Bookery agreed to provide a $25 gift certificate to be spent in store. This left one Third Prize which was provided by the Branch itself until Belinda Erikson of Empire Books stepped in. Now we were ready to set the contest in motion.

Development of the Little Details

Once the contest rules and printed flyers were available they were dropped off at each of the sponsors and all branches of the Ottawa Public Library in Gloucester, Ottawa, Nepean, Kanata and Goulbourn — time consuming but well worth the effort. That year we had over three hundred entries sent to Convener, Harry Miller. These were coded internally, with no author's name appearing on the entered poem, and judged anonymously by a qualified judge from outside the area. Honourable Mentions were permitted but with no prize.

The judge was asked to write a few lines on each winner's poem giving the reason for the choice and a brief overall comment providing the criteria used in the selection. These were read at the presentation to show how judging was done, for the benefit of the participants.

Over the years a number of members have stepped up to the plate regarding the smooth running of this contest, the branch's signature event of the year. In particular, Gill Foss, Sharyn Heagle, Louise Rachlis, Sherrill Wark, and Arlene Smith. We thank them all.

The excitement is palpable at the 24th Annual National Capital Writing Contest Awards Night while finalists, friends, and families mingle prior to the event. The awards were presented in the auditorium of the central branch of the Ottawa Public Library. Photo by Laurenzio.
(Previously published in *Byline*, Summer 2011.)

NCWC's Premier Awards Night

The first Awards Night, hosted by the President, to which all entrants were invited, was in January 1987 in the auditorium of the main branch of Ottawa Public Library. Each sponsor provided a representative to present their individual award. This was a way to thank them and indirectly promote their stores. In 1992 Bert Heward, then Books Editor for the *Ottawa Citizen*, presented First Prize awards and listed the winners in his column, announcing the Ottawa Branch of the Canadian Authors Association as behind the new contest. Some of the local winners are still actively involved today, including Sylvia Adams and Ronnie Brown.

Along with the cheque or certificate, each winner's envelope contained promotional information about CAA from National Office in the hopes of increasing membership once they recognized all the association had to offer! The winners were also given a one-year Acting Membership in the Branch until this was deemed to contravene CAA Bylaws.

Following the presentations, the first Awards Ceremony continued with non-alcoholic fruit punch along with cheese and crackers. All winners were provided with a red tag, the sponsors with green ones, so those attending could seek out whom they wished to chat with during the subsequent social time.

Evolution

As with any contest, NCWC has evolved over the years as categories, entry fees, and sponsors changed.

By 2006, the prizes for Poetry and Short Story were $250, $75 and $50, now sponsored by the *Ottawa Citizen*, by Nicholas Hoare, and by Collected Works Bookstore and Coffeebar. By the next year Nicholas Hoare had dropped out, Collected Works had taken that spot, and Read's Book Shop had joined the team with the same prize monies.

In 2008 we added a Youth Category (ages 13–17) with all prizes contributed by Dave Smith. To encourage entries, we approached all the local high schools with the result that some high quality work was produced. By this time, Collected Works Bookstore and Coffeebar had replaced the other independents although the *Ottawa Citizen* still partnered the event with the Branch contributing First

Arlene Somerton-Smith accepts her 2nd prize from Rick Davies, representing the *Ottawa Citizen* which provided second prize in each category. (Previously published in *Byline*, Summer 2010)

Prize, now increased to $500, the *Ottawa Citizen*, $250, and Collected Works Bookstore and Coffeebar, $100.

In the 2011 contest, at the suggestion of First Nations' poet and activist, Albert Dumont, for the one and only time, we set a theme, "Inspiration Planet Earth: our Natural Environment is Life" in each category and produced a well-received anthology from the encouraging results. Albert Dumont provided all First Prizes with the *Ottawa Citizen* and Collected Works covering second and third.

By 2012 the National Capital Region branch had taken over First Prize with the *Ottawa Citizen* and Collected Works Bookstore and Coffeebar sponsoring second and third, respectively. It was about this time that the *Ottawa Citizen* moved its sponsorship arm to Toronto and dropped its participation financially as well as promotionally despite the efforts of Louise Rachlis, and sadly, independent bookstores have melted away under the overwhelming pressure of Chapters/Indigo and Amazon.

From 2014 the Branch supported all prizes which were reset at $300, $200, and $100, and the entry fee increased to $15 in each of the current categories of Poetry and Short Story. This was to fall in line with other contests run by CAA branches, specifically Niagara, which competes in the same market. By 2015 we had also loosened the entry criteria to

Sherrill Wark, standing in for Christopher Smith of Collected Works Bookstore and Coffeebar, presents Véronique Hynes with her 3rd place certificate in the Youth Short Story competition. (Previously published in *Byline*, Summer 2010.)

include Quebec and all of Ontario.

The 2017 Thirtieth Anniversary NCWC Awards Night will be held in the Ottawa Public Library's central branch auditorium. It will be followed by coffee, juice and nibbles and an opportunity to chat with winners socially following the presentations. CAA–NCR has maintained the NCWC to encourage authors to contribute their work to be judged against their peers in the hope of attaining an even higher quality in their individual work. In the years to come we hope this contest will inspire new talent to reach new heights.

Paisley Laurenzio accepts her 1st Place Youth Category Award of $500 for her story, "Level One". Paisley, along with her sister, Holly — who took an Honourable Mention in this category — are home schooled. Branch President, Sharyn Heagle, presents the award. Photo by Laurenzio.
(Previously published in *Byline*, Summer 2011.)

A Member of CAA, Haiku Canada, The Ontario Poetry Society and Field Stone Poets, Gill Foss has been writing poetry since the 1980s. Many of her poems have appeared in magazines and anthologies. She has two published chapbooks: *A Window in Time* and *Fleeting Moments* and is currently working on a series of villanelles intended for a third chapbook. A full-length manuscript is in the works. She lives with three cats in rural Ontario.

Poetry

The Poetry Judge

Our Poetry Category judge, Sheila Martindale was the poetry editor for *Canadian Author* for fifteen years. She is currently editor-in-chief of *Island Writer*, the magazine of the Victoria Writers' Society. The most recent of her ten books of poetry is *Death of a Seagull*.

Sheila was a theatre reviewer for *Scene Magazine* in London, Ontario, from 1989 to 2008; she now reviews theatre for *Monday Magazine on Line* in Victoria, where snow is the cherry blossoms that fall on the sidewalks in February. She facilitates a weekly writing workshop at her local seniors' centre.

1st, 2nd and 3rd Place Poems

Gunda
by Ruth Latta

Gunda the six year old German Shepherd
tears down the hillside
then stops on the shore
to wait for the go-ahead
from the girl carrying her leash.

"It's O.K. Go in," the girl says
and Gunda springs into the water
and paddles,
kicking up silvery bubbles,
snorting when the water gets in her nose,
then stops for a rest in the shallows,
legs submerged,
surrounded by the water's green dappled circles,
framed by tall trees
with orange lilies at the base.

She finds a chunk of wood,
then lets it go and swims some more.
She never goes beyond her depth,
just back and forth between shore and float,
harmless as the blue dragon flies
that glide overhead.

Her bliss delights us.
Then a park official comes by
and says, "There's a leash law".
The girl calls to Gunda
and slowly they climb the path
and disappear from sight.

Judge's Comment

This four-stanza, seemingly simple poem, written in a conversational style, packs a lot of punch! A girl and her dog are having fun and exercise on the beach; both are loving every moment, and delighting the other people out for a stroll. The descriptions of the dog swimming for a stick are beautiful. The appearance of a park official brings the charming scene to an abrupt close. Everybody loses. A well-constructed poem which touches our emotions subtly and deeply.

About Ruth Latta

Ruth Latta's latest book is the novel *Grace and the Secret Vault* (Ottawa, Baico, 2017) Her poetry has appeared in a number of periodicals and chapbooks and also in her novel *The Songcatcher and Me* (2013).

For more information about her writing, visit
http://ruthlattabooks.blogspot.com or
http://ruthlatta.blogspot.com.

Anne from Toronto
by Ruth Latta

You came to us from Toronto.
You wore a red suit and matching lipstick
on a mouth too mobile
for a Mona Lisa smile.

In 1959.
when your high boots
first scaled our snowbanks
you must have been all of twenty-four.

On winter mornings.
in that refrigerator of a school bus
I played a movie in my head
with kings and queens of England
swishing their ermine robes
or clanking their armour —
images you created in thin air.

I yearned to be you,
full of spirit, self-esteem.

Teachers from "away"
never stayed long.
Far too soon.
you caught the Ontario Northland
back to Toronto
and your fiance.

Anne. I know now
that those china poodles I gave you
as a farewell gift were awful,
but they were the only thing in the store
that remotely suited your glamour.

I think now of your cigarettes
stained with cupid's bows
and shake my head.
In those days,
we fools thought smoking was.
 sophisticated.

Wherever you are.
you probably still wear
your wide red smile.

Judge's Comment

A wonderful poem, written long after the event, about a schoolgirl and her crush on a teacher who came, spread glamour in a northern Ontario town, and then was gone. The writer is older and wiser, and could now see the young woman in a clearer light, but she has not lost the magic of that long-ago year. Written in a casual way, the poet makes us feel as she did in 1959.

(See pg. 17 for Bio.)

Sunset
(for Gwen)
by Gill Foss

The fragility of her life fluttered as
a falling leaf caught
in a shaft of sunlight.

She walked a tightrope
over the abyss without a safety net
balancing hope and denial.

Belief in trust leaves words unsaid
and all our little lamps of hope died down
the night she breathed her last.

The dead have found a way to float
into our mind's eye unannounced.
The dead are never quiet:

with dappled sunlight filtered through the drape
of memory I hear her still
whispering old dreams.

Continued

With our gathering to celebrate
her life, that day we said goodbye to
the last setting of her sun.

Judge's Comment
This is a lovely tribute to a person who died young (or at least not old). Carefully written in economical three-line stanzas, the strong emotion is just below the surface, yet leaves one in no doubt about the pain. Skilful and elegant, this poem surprises us with its strength.

About Gill Foss
A Member of CAA, Haiku Canada, The Ontario Poetry Society and Field Stone Poets, Gill Foss has been writing poetry since the 1980s. Many of her poems have appeared in magazines and anthologies. She has two published chapbooks: *A Window in Time* and *Fleeting Moments* and is currently working on a series of villanelles intended for a third chapbook. A full-length manuscript is in the works. She lives in rural Ontario with three cats.

Honourary Mentions in Alphabetical Order

A small grief
by Bev Chambers

It was just a little thing
And yet somehow it wasn't too small to mean a lot.
The flat cap pulled down,
stylishly worn
in a way my father never could have.
Reminding me.

You think your grieving is over
when some small thing shoots you back into a maelstrom of feeling.
It could be a turn of phrase.
Or wondering what he would think of his great granddaughter,
to whom I recite rhymes
using all the different voices as my father did to me.
Watching her smile with delight, arms twirling with excitement.

It is the little things that catch me unaware.
Walking around the neighbourhood, listening to the birds,
and remembering my father whistling to the cardinals,
excited when they called back.

Over the years one thinks the grief has lessened
When suddenly it grabs you by the throat, pinning you to the wall,
leaving you gasping for air.
Until you realize, if you relax and embrace it grief will wrap its arms around you,
and comfort you in its memories.

Judge's Comment
"A Small Grief": This is a rather lovely poem, wherein the author remembers her/his father, and the little things which bring remembrances and grief flooding back. A surprising and satisfying twist at the end.

About Bev Chambers
Bev Chambers is a maternal/child nurse who worked in British Columbia, New Brunswick, the Yukon and Scotland before settling in southeastern Ontario. Her creative non-fiction stories have been published in a variety of media. She recently started writing poetry, inspired during her walks by the lake and by fellow members of her writing group. Bev is the mother of two strong daughters and Grammy to one lively granddaughter. She lives with her husband and his radio collection.

Relay
by Lee Ann Smith

Summer 2016:
Olympic Games in Rio and
I am struck by the
Hand-offs and the handing over.
Of course
The baton in track and field
And
The 4-by-100 team swim
But also
The old guard naming the new guard
Usain Bolt about Andre De Grasse:
"He'll be the next fastest man."

In Olympic competition
There is always faster, higher, farther.

Summer 2016:
I feel the pool's edge against my fingertips
Breathless

My lap complete
I am instantly shadowed by my sons diving over me.
They butterfly away
Take their lap.
On the far end of the pool, the next swimmers
Tense
On toes
Wait for the instant my boys touch the edge.

In families
There is always a breathlessly fast swim towards the new guard.

Judge's Comment
"Relay": The 2016 Olympics remind a spectator that there is always someone running at the heels of an athlete, someone who will be better and who will catch up and overtake the star. Same thing in families …

About Lee Ann Smith
Lee Ann Smith's passion for history and storytelling has driven her writing career. She is the author of two acclaimed non-fiction history books, along with many magazine articles about how to write family history and memoir. In the past few years, she's returned to her love of writing poetry and has also discovered a new passion: taking pictures of beautiful things she finds in her everyday world. She's currently working on her second collection of poetry inspired by these photographs.

Too Long a Winter
by Lee Ann Smith

Through the kitchen window
spring air
caresses like fingertips on a cheek
.
Spring air
scented with earth
as if soil particles thawed and dissolved into it
made it more complex than what it once was:

Winter air
clear, empty, vast
without content.

The air has melted.
A new season pulses
sap and blood on the rise, while

We sit silently at the kitchen table
frozen like winter air
our conversation polite
without content.

Hearts, like air, can melt.
But has it been too long a winter?

Judge's Comment
"Too Long a Winter": An interesting look at the season of spring after a long winter. Does the same thawing apply to human beings? Nicely put.

(See pg. 25 for Bio.)

Short Stories

The Short-Story Judge

Matthew Bin holds a BA and MA in English literature from McMaster University. He has worked as a technical writer, business/systems analyst, and consultant with numerous public- and private-sector clients for nearly 20 years.

Matthew's first novel, *L.M.F.*, was published by Little Green Tree Books in 2006, and his first non-fiction book, *On Guard for Thee: Canadian Peacekeeping Missions*, was published by Bookland Press in 2007. He has published articles in numerous magazines, including *In Burlington*, *The Windsor Review*, and *Inside Soccer Canada*. He won a Hamilton ACE Award in 2003 in the Marketing Writing category. He is currently the Canadian Football Editor for the popular sports website *LastWordOnSports.com*, bassist and backup shouter for a punk rock band, and a licensed marriage officiant.

As a member of the Board of Directors for the Canadian

Authors Association, Matthew has served as President of the Waterloo-Wellington branch, Strategic Planning Chair, Recording Secretary, Treasurer, Membership Chair, and National Chair. He also serves as the Secretary of the Canadian Copyright Institute.

Matthew's next book, *Brendan's Way*, will be published by Bundoran Press in 2017.

1st, 2nd and 3rd Place Short Stories

The Flower Seller of Agra
by Shiela Jane

My name is Anjuli. I sell flowers on the road that leads to the Taj Mahal. In the morning, when there are fewer tourists, I sit in the sand and look at that new white palace shining in the sun, and remember. I am an old woman now, and penniless, but once I lived in the Court of Kings.

That was the Golden Age, a time when the Empire was blessed beyond all other countries of the world, when the line of the Mughal emperors was strong, and the people of India were happy. Love made it so.

The prince Khurram — Shah Jahan, as he was later known — was betrothed to Arjumand when she was just fourteen. Yet for years, he had not seen her. Then one morning he chose to walk in the market square and chanced upon his bride to be, bargaining the price of silks like a common housewife. I was her servant. I was with her that day and saw him looking at us as we laughed and talked with the vendors and the shoppers. He followed us home and kept watching from the garden. As I removed her veil, the breeze coming in through the windows blew her long hair into her eyes, and she brushed her hand through it. It was like a raven unfolding its wings for flight. I saw that Khurram could not take his eyes off her.

That evening, he sent his man to bring her to him. The valet came to me and I told Arjumand that the prince desired her presence and had sent her a nightingale as a gift. She looked at the bird in its golden cage and said, "Am I to be like this poor creature?" Then she took it out of the cage and let it fly through the open window.

The valet went back without the bird and without Arjumand. I trembled at the thought of the prince's anger, feared for my lady's life ... and her servant's as well. Soldiers would be at the door at any moment, I expected.

But it was Jahan himself who came. He stepped into the drawing room that was so dainty and feminine, like Arjumand herself, and overwhelmed it with his energy. He bowed to my mistress and said, "You released my nightingale, yet *I* am the captive one." Then he kissed her hand and knelt at her feet.

From that day, she was destined to be the jewel in Jahan's crown. He married her and called her Mumtaz Mahal. He was besotted with his new wife. Two other wives he had already, and children; they were all but forgotten. Everything he did now became an offering to this new wife, this *girl*, who commanded his life with nothing more than a smile. The building of massive forts, changes to the court, even military conquests — everything he did was *for* her.

I lived with her at the Royal Court. We were much the same age and as like as twin sisters in feature, although so different in fact. It is a mysterious thing, beauty. How the same eyes, the same mouth, the same curve of face and slightness of build can translate into such unique aspects in two different women, how what is so plain in one can be illuminated somehow into true loveliness in the other. Mumtaz was the perfect pearl created by a divine hand. I was simply the reflection in the mirror.

My duties were not onerous. I was her companion, her confidante, and in some ways her protector. For life at court was not peaceful. There was fury among the rest of the royal family at being deposed from Jahan's affections so thoughtlessly.

As I quickly learned, political wives wield their power in subtle ways — through quiet alliances, by currying the affection of servants, and with maternal influence.

Mumtaz was shunned by many, but her love for Jahan kept her head high. When he was at the palace, no one could touch her. But when he was away … oh then, the blades were sharpened more openly. There was one in particular who watched with needles in her eyes — Nur, a wife of Jahan's father, Jahangir, and the real power behind the throne.

"I fear her, Anjuli," Mumtaz said to me many times. "She knows that Jahan is strong and will one day soon become King, and then her power will be gone. She will do anything to stop me from replacing her as the chosen queen."

I soothed her, saying, "My lady, you're tired and imagining things. No one could wish you ill." But I knew as she did that Nur was dangerous.

Still, the love of Jahan and my mistress became stronger year by year and they had many children together. He could not keep away from her and no sooner did Mumtaz bring forth one baby than its successor was on the way. As their family grew, so did Jahan's power and accomplishments in the battle field. He began to be restless to take his father's place as the supreme ruler, and on many occasions, the voices of the two men could be heard raised in anger over some disagreement.

One day when Mumtaz was nearing the birth of yet another

child, she walked with me by the stone palace wall. We talked of her hope that this latest confinement would produce a son again, and of how Jahan was even now impatient to return to her bed. We reached the steep staircase carved into the wall leading to the garden and paused to look down at the lilies and bougainvillea blooming below.

"I will pick the best for you," I said and ran down to gather the flowers.

Just as I reached the cool grass, there was a cry from above, not a long scream, just a sharp shriek like that of a fox run to ground. I turned to see Mumtaz tumbling down the rough sandstone steps toward me.

I must have fainted, because all I remember of the rest of that night is the sense of pain and grief. For the baby was lost. Even now, so many years later, I mourn for the precious life that never was. There were other babies that did not live, but it is that one I dream of, it is that one that I'm remembering when I wake sometimes in the middle of the night with tears flowing down my checks.

Jahan was beside himself. Not just because of the miscarriage, but because Mumtaz clung to him that night, weeping and repeating over and over, "Khurram ... *she* did it. She pushed me, tried to *kill* me! I cannot go on like this."

There was no real proof that the fall was caused by Nur's hand. But it was enough for Jahan that Mumtaz said it to be the truth. And when Jahangir angrily dismissed the suggestion, the rift between father and son became war. What happened then is now part of the history of the Empire.

Nur was cunning enough to know that if she lost this battle, she would lose her very freedom. Under the guise of wifely advice, she marshaled the Mughal forces against Jahan in the most ferocious manner and though his men fought bravely they were vanquished.

It was only by the grace of Jahangir that Jahan and my lady were spared the sword. Yet Nur was not satisfied. She began a new and devastating campaign — a secret friendship with their third son, Aurangzeb, who was now a young man.

What devilish ideas she put into his head, turning him against his own parents and older brothers with promises of wealth and power far beyond his natural claim. If only Jahan had taken more interest in his children's progress. If only Mumtaz had remained at home with them instead of accompanying her beloved husband on his travels. If only …

***

The end of the love story came with little warning. Jahan had finally become the Emperor following the death of his father and had immediately imprisoned Nur. In 1631, he was fighting a campaign in the Deccan Plateau and Mumtaz was with him, and with child again. I was there too by her side. She was happier than she had ever been now that her sworn enemy had been declawed. Or so she thought.

When the birthing pains began, I held Mumtaz's hands and we prayed together. As we were kneeling on the mat, a water girl came and touched my shoulder.

"A man is here," she whispered. "He looks like a beggar, but his speech is like a noble. And he came by horse. He asks for an urgent audience with the Queen about her son."

I was shaking my head but Mumtaz heard and said, "What is that? What son? Bring him!"

The water girl went away and came back with a tall turbaned young man. He was clearly exhausted and covered in the dust of travel. One sleeve was torn and the arm underneath was wrapped in a stained and torn bandage.

He practically fell at my feet — at *Mumtaz's* feet — and cried, "My Queen, a thousand pardons for disturbing your peace. But there is great danger on the way. My name is Nawaz. I am a guardian of the palace. I have word from the prison that your son, Aurangzeb, has been plotting with Queen Nur against Shah Jahan. They plan to take over the Peacock Throne and kill both Jahan and you, while you are here, far away from the court. Aurangzeb sent this message to his Horse Master but I intercepted it." He held out his hand and showed her a waslis, a parchment with the words in calligraphy faint but legible.

Mumtaz crumbled before my eyes. She would not have believed it of her own son, but the words were there in the hand of a court calligrapher, the directives to the Horse Master a proof she could not dismiss. She would have fallen with shock and the pain of the babe about to be born if Nawaz had not caught her.

We placed her on her bed and I sent Nawaz away. I could not stop crying at the thought of what Nur had brought about, the bitterness that she had cultivated so long and so carefully in Aurangzeb. So artfully she would have suggested Jahan's favouritism toward his older sons and the supposed injustices done to Nur herself. So subtly, she must have dropped veiled hints of Mumtaz's infidelities and her belief that he, Aurangzeb, was the true heir to the throne.

"It will not end until death itself ends it," I said.

Mumtaz knew it was the truth. She had intelligence, if I may be permitted to say that myself. Intelligence and a will that matched that of her archenemy, Queen Nur. In that long night while she laboured to give life to her child, she also gave birth to a plan.

She held my hands and said over and over. "It is because of me that Nur has done this, because of her hatred and jealousy. She can stop Aurangzeb but she won't do it until I am dead. That is the only thing that will cool her anger.

"Anjuli, you can see that, can't you? You understand. If I were to die tonight, the country would go into mourning. Jahan would halt the campaign and return to the palace. Aurangzeb and Nur could get away with assassinating him on the battlefield, but not while he is surrounded by a wall of supporters and loyal subjects. Their plot would be found out and they themselves would be put to death. You must help me, Anjuli, *tonight*. For Jahan's sake, you must do as I ask."

***

The rest you know through the history books. Mumtaz Mahal did die that night … in childbirth … at least that is what the court scribes wrote. There are … were … only a few people who knew the truth. Most have gone to the holy place by now.

The doctor who prepared her body, the trusted servants who covered her face in the burial shroud, the one who opened the gate for me when I left in the early hours of morning, I swore them all to secrecy. Jahan himself never knew. His grief is there for the world to see in the white tomb that is his finest achievement.

Now, so many years later, Jahan himself is gone. Aurangzeb is Emperor. And I? I sit here in the sand selling flowers and look upon the Taj Mahal. In the moonlight, it glows with the sheen of a pearl.

Mumtaz had intelligence and strong will, as I have said. But in the end, she did not have the courage.

No! Just this once, let me speak as myself, as the Queen I once was. *I* did not have courage. Try to understand when I say, I loved my little Anjuli. She was my dearest friend. I did not *want* to do what I did. Yet, when the time came to make that final sacrifice, I was afraid. I could not let go of life. Instead I exchanged one life for another. She was terrified, but I told her she would live forever in the world beyond this one. It was her duty to obey. We wept together even as I held the soft woollen blanket over her face.

So that night, my little servant girl — the reflection of the jewel in the mirror — *became* the perfect pearl. She is there still in the tomb Jahan built for me, that memorial to eternal love. .

And now … my name is Anjuli. I am a flower seller. But once, I lived in the Court of Kings.

Judge's Comment

Palace intrigue in an exotic setting beguiles the reader as they are revealed by a simple handmaiden. We're quickly caught up in the tale of Jahan and his canny bride Mumtaz, beset on all sides by rivals for the Emperor's throne. But as the story twists and turns toward its end, the narrative voice breaks suddenly and dramatically — and we're left to pick up the pieces. An excellent piece of storytelling that lingers long after the story is done.

About Shiela Jane

Shiela Jane was born in Mumbai, India, and lived there for several years before moving to Quebec and later Ontario. She holds a degree in political science and diploma in journalism and also studied creative writing. Her work has been published in a variety of magazines, newspapers, and fiction anthologies. *The Saltwater Ghost* is her first novel.

California Pure
by Elle Wild

The earth is cracked like giant scales, but the empty creek bed is a dragon's tail that I am following. The snap of my dusty flip-flops is the rattle of claws, the rumbling in my stomach, his roar. This is my favourite part of the day: the time I spend foraging. Before the drought, I'd find lush fiddleheads here, *Pteretis pensylvanica,* their tender curls like tiny snails. And especially wild mushrooms. Back when I could still find *Cantharellus californicus*, my golden frilled mud puppies, I'd sell chanterelles to Café Carbonero. Sometimes we sold to New Leaf, the organic grocery store where Mom works. But now, no water means no mushrooms. And we can't afford the groceries in New Leaf. Soon enough, no one will be able to. This thought makes me glance at the heavens, dreaming of dark, ragged clouds like bats. But the sky is a cruel cobalt. No rain today.

Grandpa Leo will cook whatever I manage to find. He's the one who taught me how to tell the difference between a morel and a false morel. Today it's mostly nettles, which are good for making tea — if you've got water — but not for filling your belly. Still, hunger isn't our biggest problem. It's the thirsty people that worry me, the armed ones we hear about on Leo's radio. I know that things will get worse before they get better. Mom doesn't like me in the woods on my own anymore, but when she smokes the crumbly leaves, she forgets. And I'm always careful. I listen for the telltale snapping of twigs, for the hard sound of men's boots over the green song of California bush crickets. Besides, we have to eat.

I press deeper into the forest, farther away from the dry streambed. The medicinal scent of eucalyptus envelops me, but I move quickly through the sunlit grove. The fallen leaves and pine needles are brown and brittle: thousands of little matches waiting to ignite. Eucalyptus is good for making natural healing oils and insecticides, but it's fussy work to distil them and they're a common leaf, so the price isn't good. I carry on, into the darkness of pine and oak. That's where you find what I'm looking for. One of the things, anyway. I move toward an earthier smell of decay. There's a fallen oak tree that may have what I want. It does. At first I think it's *Amanita velosa*, because of the lovely parasol shape. Then I realize my mistake.

The smaller of the two mushrooms is so perfectly smooth and dick-shaped that it grabs my attention. It's paler than it should be — not the speckled brown and cream of a hen's egg. This one is pure white. Then I see the universal veil and the bulbous bit at the bottom, where the toxins pool. This isn't *Amanita velosa*. It's *Amanita virosa*, "The Destroying Angel". My favourite mushroom name. Since I started reading my father's Bible, I've been really into the idea of angels. Leo says that Bible stories are just a way to explain the world, like Greek Mythology, or any stories for that matter. Still, this Bible is the only thing my father left behind when he left us to go on tour, and I find it a comfort to hold some little piece of my father inside my head until I find him again. So I'll keep my angels.

The petticoat of the big *Virosa* has a proud look about it, like flapping wings, and I *have* to pick it. Might be the closest I ever come to an angel, even if it's an angel of death. I lift the white meat of the thing gently in my cupped hand — like raising a glass of wine to make a toast, according to Leo. Then I slip its soft form into the crumpled paper bag inside my backpack. Leo says everything is valuable in good time; it's just a matter of hanging on to it until you find the right buyer. There may be dark days ahead, so every little thing is precious. And anyway, it's good to know that if Poppy annoys me more than I can really stand, I can always do her in. I reckon it's good to have options.

When I emerge into the burning light of our yard, Leo is in the pickup with the windows rolled down, already running the engine. Poppy is sitting in the back, giving me a *look*. Poppy is four years older than me and has shoulder-length *brown* hair. It's a shame that Mom had already used the name, because my hair is bright orange, the colour of *Eschscholzia californica* — a California poppy — but I got stuck with "Clematis".

Poppy says I should be glad, because Mom almost named me Wyethia or Ithuriel. I would rather be Wyethia, or especially Ithuriel, which might be a flower to Mom, but to me, Ithuriel is Gabriel's angel — the one who wielded a spear and smote Satan with the tip. Ithuriel sounds powerful. It sounds like my father, Michael, and the archangel in his left-behind Bible. Though Leo says "Michael" means "poor" and is apt since my father's band, The Monk Daddies, all went bankrupt. That's the reason he disappeared and stopped making support payments, Mom says, with that contracted look about her mouth.

Leo winks and revs the engine, his huge eyes the changing colours of water. Leo has silver-white hair that is still quite long. Like any of the old surfers you see around Santa Cruz. But it's his eyes that hold your attention, even when he's rambling on about his personal journey to Tibet or India in the 1970s. He's getting hairier about his eyebrows and nose, though. I can't decide whether or not to tell him. It's probably best that I don't. Leo talks about making changes, but I know that some changes aren't for the better, which is why we have to do what we are about to do. No matter how much Poppy might object.

***

Voices rise like the heat off the asphalt we're sitting on, here in this concrete desert, wedged between a parking lot and a Costco store in downtown Santa Cruz. Oily wafts of sunscreen and greasy rotisserie chicken mingle with something else. Fear, perhaps.

The chicken smell cuts through me. They still sell it inside, but we can't afford it anymore. Prices have skyrocketed, although that isn't what the crowd is shouting about. This is about water. California's water, taken from the Santa Cruz Mountains.

Behind us, in the window, is the reason we are here — five gallon bottles of water with a sign that reads, *California PURE Spring Water: Pure Life.* They don't dare show the price in public. Leo says that we shouldn't have let them take our water in the middle of a drought; now the community reserve is dry. Our well is almost dry, too.

The lineup for water goes all the way down the sidewalk we are sitting on, but those buying are still outnumbered by those with angry signs. Looking at all the anxious faces, I feel more skittish than I have since The Great Drought began. Some of these people may be armed. Maybe all of them. We have only our placards, and my hidden angel, but no one knows about that — and little good it would do against the things people keep hidden. I know what happens when people here start opening their purses.

I keep my head down — looking at my dirty feet and breathing the scorching air. Leo holds his placard high and shouts, "California PURE, purveyors of pure drought! Free water for everyone!" in his baritone voice, then wipes his brow. He says it's our democratic right to protest and we should be proud we still have it, even though half of the country are right-wing rednecks and morally bankrupt.

Leo has some kooky ideas, like the one about Dead-Granny-Lorna being our guardian angel. Leo thinks that Lorna is the real reason that his old television gave up the ghost at the outset of the water shortage: Dead-Granny didn't want us watching the news all the time to see how bad things would get. The gangs of thirsty men forcing their way into the wealthy homes along West Cliff. Still, it may be a little loco, but this guardian idea appeals to me as I scan the lineup. Read the faces.

I glance at Poppy who has a faraway look in her eye like she's just biding her time. At sixteen, she's mastered the art of being in a place without actually being there. Leo accuses her of "not being present", but sometimes I envy her.

A commotion at the window catches my eye. Inside, the last jugs of water are being handed down, and the crowd behind the glass swells. There's a tug of war at the bottle closest to me, then behind the sloshing water, I glimpse something that I've lost and have been searching for. My father.

At least, I think it's Michael, but he doesn't look the way he does in pictures, with long hair and a leather jacket. Now, his auburn hair is short and he's wearing a shirt with a *PURE California* logo. I've always thought of Michael as one of my guardian angels, like Dead-Granny-Lorna: out there protecting me, even if I can't see him. If he isn't here, then it must be Mom's fault, because someone with a name like Michael has to be good. Michael's mouth falls open and I swear he sees me, but I must be mistaken because he turns away, and is obscured by the surge of bodies and the storm in the bottle. I have to find him. I'm on my feet now but before I can reach Michael, Leo grabs me by the wrist, tugging me away from the heave and sway of the crowd as the first shot is fired.

***

Back at home, I leave Leo with his radio and his solemn expression, and find my way back to the dank, leafy place that smells of death, where the pure white mushrooms grow. I sit on the decaying oak and let my thoughts settle. I wonder how many days of freedom I have left in my forest. Leo says not to worry — we have enough water in the well to last a few more days. What he doesn't say is, "until they come for it." There's a prickling sensation like dry spikes of pine needles inside me, and they feel like they're about to combust when I think that Michael is working nearby and just isn't helping us.

What was I expecting? For Michael to hold me while we mourned our lost years together? For him to keep all of the thirsty people at bay? The rage surges from all of the tight corners where I've buried it. Shhh, I tell myself. *Shhh*.

A nearby branch tickles my cheek. Without thinking, I bend and twist the twig until it snaps. It's a "Y" shape, with remnants of leaves still clinging to it. I pull them off. A foolish idea occurs to me, something Leo told me once about what Dead-Granny-Lorna was able to do with a piece of willow. This isn't willow, but I try it anyway. I begin walking. About ten paces along, I feel something strange. It's like a tingling at first. The awareness of a life force pulling below the earth's surface. Then it's stronger, a magnet yanking my stick down. I couldn't resist even if I wanted to, and I don't, because this changes everything.

When I tell them, there is silence. First about Michael, and then about my power. Mom's eyebrows raise and her mouth opens, but nothing comes out. "Prove it," Poppy says.

***

I've brought the stick that worked before, but now I feel doubt. I see myself reflected in the dark sunglasses of the others. What they see: a weedy, freckled kid in a dirty baseball cap. Not mighty Ithuriel. I glance at my mother's face, read the hope that's written there, too, softening the fine lines of her sunburned face.

It's eerily quiet, like nature is plotting something. At ten paces, there's no water. I rub a hand over my belly to relax the tension I'm carrying there. Leo coughs. I swallow dryly. I can't help thinking about the thirsty people with guns who might take our water, and this makes my throat constrict even more. Forty paces. It's not going to happen.

A few more steps and I feel it. It's a dark, rushing feeling, like the lifeblood inside me. I know what direction it's flowing. I can tell the depth beneath the surface: it's deeper this time.

Leo digs where I tell him to. For a while, there's just the whispered shhhh shhhh tone of the shovel, like the quashing of a secret. We're all afraid to say anything, to break the spell. The *What if I'm wrong? What if I'm right?* pattern of metal in earth. We wait for the joyful gurgling sound that will fill Leo's shovel, for the mirth of that imagined sound to spill over onto our faces.

Judge's Comment

Who knew post-apocalyptic tales could be so horrifying? The world in this story is built deftly and carefully, which heightens the emotional impact of the story as it drives towards its unresolved but satisfying conclusion. Every word of the story seems carefully and artfully chosen.

About Elle Wild

Elle Wild grew up in a dark, rambling farmhouse in the wilds of Canada where there was nothing to do but read Edgar Allan Poe and watch PBS mysteries. She is an award-winning short filmmaker and the former writer/host of the radio program Wide Awake on CBC Radio One. Her short fiction has been published in Ellery Queen Magazine and her articles have appeared in The Toronto Star, Georgia Straight, Whitehorse Daily Star and Westender. Wild's debut novel, Strange Things Done, won the Arthur Ellis Award 2015 for Best Unpublished First Crime Novel, and was shortlisted in multiple contests internationally. In 2017, Strange Things Done made the #1 Amazon Best Seller list in Canada for Noir. Women in Film & Television Vancouver have just announced that Wild is one of five winners in its "From Our Dark Side" genre writing contest for screen.

Recently returned from the U.K., Wild currently resides on an island in the Salish Sea named after the bones of dead whales.

Extra Innings
by Jeff Shiau

Top of the first

Baseball is a game of patience. There is no clock. In the outfield, half the game might pass before a ball is hit your way. But when it comes, you need to be quick: to pounce on that line drive, to track down that fly ball.

I met Ike in Little League. I played centrefield, he played right. Nice guy, but badass too, the kind of kid my parents wanted me to steer clear of. He shoplifted and swore. He was fast and loose with his money. Maybe that's why I liked him. Me, I was goody two-shoes, I did my homework. Maybe that's why he liked me.

It was the mid-1980s: a time of big sweaters and skinny jeans. I was a year younger than Ike. I never thought someone like him, would be interested in someone like me. He helped me loosen up, to see the world from a different perspective. That's why it hurt so much the day I said we couldn't be friends.

Second inning

Our friendship started innocently. After getting to know each other on the diamond, we'd hang out after a game, grab a slushie or play some Atari. We were an odd pair, badass with goody two-shoes. He didn't care what people thought. I admired that.

Ike had a paper route and proposed sharing it with me. Gave us a bit of pocket change. We went to different schools, so after class, whoever got to the drop-off first would start deliveries.

To get our "collect" money, we had to knock on customers' doors — they'd pay us directly, then Ike would submit the funds to his supervisor. We met all kinds of characters along the route. "Try not to laugh at this guy," Ike warned, as we approached a customer's apartment. I rapped on the door. Slowly, it swung open, revealing a bleary-eyed, skinny Chinese dude in his tighty-whities. Dang.

"Collect," I said, as we tried our best not to burst out laughing. Dude stretched and yawned, paid, shut the door.

"What the hell was that?" I asked. "Does he always answer the door in his gitch?"

"Every time," Ike quipped. "Lester Molester."

Sometimes we'd blow our collect money on freezies at the corner store. We pigged out on a lot of them, with the brain freezes to show for it.

Third inning

Baseball is a game of turns. One team bats while the other is in the field. Good friends take turns. They learn to compromise, to try new things. Ike was good at getting me to do that. But from my perspective, it didn't really work in reverse. At times, I felt we only did the things he wanted to. Granted, some of it was thrilling: stealing alcohol from our parents' liquor cabinets, shoplifting at the corner store. Maybe I was infatuated with the idea of hanging with a "cool" kid. The excitement blinded me; it was almost like we were dating. A "bromance", before the term was coined. Maybe that's why I cut him some slack. We did some things I wasn't too proud of. But at twelve years old, peer pressure was a bitch.

Fourth inning

"Hey," Ike said one day as we watched TV, "have you ever been in a fight?"

"No," I replied, confused as to where this was leading.

"It's fun, you should try it."

"What are you talking about?" I asked incredulously. Ike explained any frustrations we had in life could evaporate if we occasionally beat up on each other. How primal.

"Sounds stupid," I said.

"Just try it," he prodded, giving me a friendly jab. I reluctantly exchanged a few half-hearted punches, but then he caught me with a good one. What the heck? Pissed off, I let loose. Soon we were brawling. We made it a regular occurrence: our own little Fight Club. Every now and then, we kicked the crap out of each other. Crazily, it felt good — this infliction and receipt of pain; a strange and visceral pleasure. Man, it was so wack.

What was happening? I was a strait-laced Taiwanese kid who took piano lessons and got straight A's. Heck, I was twelve years old and had Canada Savings Bonds. Suddenly, I was pilfering booze, shoplifting and fighting. Part of me loved it, but another part recognized I was straying from who I was: good kid, not badass.

Fifth inning

When Ike and I practised pitching, we fancied ourselves Blue Jay aces, like Jimmy Key or Dave Stieb. Throwing the ball around one day, Ike asked, "Why are you so stingy with your money?"

Pop! went the ball into my glove. "Whaddya mean?" I asked.

Ike said I was cheap, that I was always reluctant to dole out the dinero. *Curveball.*

I argued that's the way I was brought up, to be a saver. I felt compelled to defend how I was raised. Also felt like Ebenezer Scrooge.

Screw you. *Fastball.*

He questioned the point of having money if you never spent it. There was a certain logic to his argument. *Changeup.* I loosened up a bit with the purse strings.

Sixth Inning

We'd hang in my basement sometimes. We had an original IBM PC, a ping pong table and a vintage '70s TV, encased in wood. Shooting the breeze in our "boy cave", Ike asked if I knew what blood brothers were.

"Uh, sort of … not really," I answered. He explained the concept of a blood oath; two people cutting themselves, then pressing their wounds together, solidifying their bond.

"Do you wanna do it?" he asked. I was unsure. Sounded weird, but alluring.

The needle pricked our palms, only hurt a bit. A few seconds passed; blood ran. We shook hands. He looked me in the eye and said "now we're brothers."

Oddly exciting, knowing our blood ran through each other's veins.

Ike was always proposing different things. Things I never would have thought of. Before him, my life was school, sports, piano; hanging out with my little brother and neighbour. I felt bad I didn't hang with them as much. But I was in Junior High. Weren't you supposed to make new friends?

Seventh inning

I shared a bedroom with my brother. Dark brown carpet, walls plastered with Blue Jay idols cut out from magazines, newspapers. One afternoon, Ike and I were reading some comics or something. I sat on my bed; he sat across from me on my brother's. Out of the blue, he invited me to his side and asked, "You wanna snuggle?"

Huh? I felt apprehensive, not having come from a family of snugglers.

"I don't know … it's kind of weird."

"I'm not friggin' gay," Ike countered, "if that's what you're worried about." He argued as little kids, we didn't think anything of snuggling with our parents or a sibling. Chicks do it; why should it be different for us when we're older?

Seemed sensible enough, I guess. We crawled under the covers and lay beside each other, talking about stuff like girls we had crushes on, or the Jays' post-season prospects. That's all it ever was. Nothing more, nothing less. Peaceful.

Until my mom walked in, aghast. "What are you doing?" she asked.

"Uh … we're just talking, Mom," I said, embarrassed, as we got out from under the blankets.

That night, my mom asked if Ike ever touched me.

"Mom!" I exclaimed, taken aback, "please! We don't do anything. We just … talk." She didn't understand our snuggling was a platonic act. Well, that's how I saw it, at least.

"I don't think it's a good idea," she said. "What if he is homosexual?"

"Mom!" I yelled, "he's not gay! And if he was, who cares?!"

"Do you think you should be friends with him?" she asked, with motherly concern. "I don't know if he is such a good boy."

"Gimme a break, Mom. You're worried for nothing."

Seventh inning stretch

Christmas season. We were downtown at the Rideau Centre, looking for gifts. Adolescents liked to hang at the food court. Some looked for trouble, others looked to stay out of it. We slurped some Orange Julius, people-watching. You know, the usual suspects: preps, mods, skaters, jocks. We left the food court and started browsing.

Ike slid some merchandise into his pockets. "What the hell are you doing?" I said, alarmed. This wasn't the corner store anymore. Ike had moved up to the big leagues. He fashioned his own sale: *Five-finger discount. Get it while quantities last.*

Shoplifting is pretty easy. The trick is to act naturally. If you're nervous, you'll probably give yourself away. Walk around like you own the joint, but don't get too greedy. You have to do your homework. Notice the staff's routines. A partner can distract while the other does the lifting.

I didn't feel very natural, though. My heart pounded with every item I swiped. I knew it was wrong, but didn't speak up. Peer pressure — my worst enemy. I could have said: "No, Ike, I'm not doing this!" Would he still have wanted to be my friend? Probably. But I was too chicken to stand up for myself.

We stashed our goods in a locker and kept going back for more. Greedy. Must have stolen from at least six or seven different stores. Our Christmas "shopping" was almost done. *Home run,* or so we thought. We hadn't noticed a man tailing us. A big man. In a dark blue uniform. When we returned to our locker, he pounced. *Strikeout.*

The security guard led us into the bowels of the mall, twisting and turning, as we ominously awaited our fate. The police were called. Our families too. When my dad walked in, I had never felt so ashamed.

We got off with a very stern warning and were banned from the mall for a year. We were lucky not to be charged. I knew my relationship with Ike would have to end. I had to work up the courage to extricate myself.

On the car ride home, not much was said. I knew I messed up. My dad was too angry or worse yet, disappointed, to say anything. He parked the car and trudged me inside.

"What were you thinking?" he scolded.

"I don't know, Dad," I shrugged. "I'm sorry."

Until then, my father had stayed silent on my friendship with Ike. Mom was the one who voiced her disapproval. They didn't have to say more; I had let them down. Worse yet, I let myself down.

Eighth inning

About a week later, the phone rang. No call display back then, but I suspected who it was. I waited a couple rings, then picked up.

"Hello."

"Hey," Ike said.

"Hey," I replied.

There was a pause. We didn't really know what to say. We hadn't talked since the incident. We compared notes on how much crap our parents gave us, and shared a few laughs. In the background, I was contemplating how to end our friendship.

"So, when do you wanna hang out?" Ike asked. I was dreading the moment and took a deep breath.

"Ike …" I said, gathering courage, "I, uh … I can't see you anymore."

"Whaddya mean?"

"I just can't. My parents won't let me."

Another pause.

"Your parents won't let you," he said, "but do *you* want to?"

My heart sank as I tried to answer; a lump formed in my throat. I steadied myself, then thought of the good times we shared, like playing ball, or laughing at skinny Chinese underwear dude. I wanted to see him, but knew he wasn't healthy for me.

"I can't, Ike."

This severing of our friendship was one of the hardest things I had ever done. Felt like a traitor.

"That's not what I asked you," he said. "Do you *want* to see me?"

Silence.

"No," I lied nervously.

An awful feeling rose from the pit of my stomach. "I *don't* want to see you, Ike —" I quivered. "I'm sorry."

I began to cry. He was quiet. I hung up.

"I'm sorry …" I whispered.

Ninth inning

The closer in baseball is a relief pitcher, often brought in the last inning, who specializes in protecting a close lead and finishing the game. Tom Henke, nicknamed "The Terminator", was the Jays' closer. If you're old enough, you might remember him from an aftershave commercial. He was the Aqua Velva Man.

I had terminated my friendship with Ike. I closed the game. Only, this wasn't a game. There was no celebration. Instead: a void.

Ike had come into my life when I really hadn't done or seen a lot. He injected excitement, and helped me to be more spontaneous and confident. He was generous with his time and friendship. We were very close. We were blood brothers.

By the time we parted, I was thirteen years old. A teenager. I didn't set boundaries or speak up for myself. Had I, we might have salvaged our friendship before it was too late. But at the time, the only way I knew to help myself was to end it — to close the game. *Screwball.*

Extra Innings

I ran into Ike a couple years later at a party. We had both matured some, but I remembered the same freckles on his face, the same middle part in his hair. We were surprised and nervous to bump into each other.

"Hey," I said.

"Hey," he replied.

We exchanged pleasantries, then smiled and didn't say anything for a while. I thought about rekindling our friendship, but couldn't bring myself to go there.

"Well …" I dithered, "take care of yourself, Ike."

"You too," he nodded. I think he wanted to say more, but like me, chose not to. We went our separate ways. I never heard from Ike again.

Judge's Comment

An artfully constructed story that follows the evolution of a childhood friendship. The author has reflected the complex relationships and rituals of two youths in a way that gets at real and honest truth. The trip back to childhood, with its very sophisticated problems, is refreshing and touching.

About Jeff Shiau

Jeff Shiau lives and works in Ottawa. His essays have appeared in *The Globe and Mail* and *The Good Men Project*. He also chronicles his adventures as a dad on his personal blog. When he's not writing, Jeff runs a freelance web design business. He enjoys playing piano, gardening and hanging out with his wife and two sons.

Honourable Mentions in Alphabetical Order

Unexpected
by Barbara Wackerle Baker

"Good morning. Accounting Department," I say into the phone. "How can I help you?"

"Hi, Mrs. G."

Oh my God. It's her. I bite my bottom lip.

"Mrs. G? Are you there?"

"Yes, Afton," I finally say. "I'm here."

"Oh, I thought I lost you like there was a bad connection or something."

"Nope, there's not a bad connection." What the hell does she want? "I'm ... surprised to hear from you."

"I know. It's been a while. Weird eh?" I hear her giggle. "Me calling you now."

"Weird? I guess you could call it that."

"Anyways, I was wondering," Afton carries on. "I'd like to take you out for coffee. We need to talk. There's something I *have* to tell you."

"Pardon?" A pulse thumps in my ear.

"Oh, Mrs. G. Relax. It's not that." She laughs. "You don't have to worry about that ever again. Can we go for coffee? I really need to talk to you. I want to, you know, explain stuff."

"I don't think there's anything left to explain, Afton. It's been a really rough summer. For all of us."

"I know. But, I'm over it. It was tough at first but, honest, I'm good. Please," she begs. "Come have coffee with me. My mom's coming too."

"Your mom is coming?" I grab a clump of permed ringlets and wind them around my finger till the roots tug my scalp. "Afton, I don't think this is a very good idea."

"Yes, it is. You'll see. Please! It's real important that I talk to you. And then, then you'll never have to see me again unless, you know, unless you want to. Okay?"

I say nothing.

"Please Mrs. G. You won't be sorry. I promise."

"Okay. Fine. Where? When?"

***

The bell jingles above the door as I enter the almost empty coffee shop. With a cup of decaf in hand, I take the corner table so I can watch who comes in.

What the hell am I doing?

I blow across the top of the cup before I take a sip. The bell jingles again. Afton and her mom walk in. The bottoms of Afton's flared jeans flap against each other as she hurries toward me.

"I knew you'd come." She turns to her mom. "See, I told you she'd come. She never lets me down."

I force a smile so big my cheeks hurt. After they grab coffee, Afton and her mom sit across from me. I wrap my hands around my warm mug and nod at them with the same stiff smile. My blouse sticks to my armpits. Afton takes a wad of pink gum out of her mouth, rolls it into a ball and sets it on a spoon. Her mom drops a napkin over it.

"I'm so glad you came. I've wanted to tell you this for months. I just didn't know how to. And Nathan, well, he didn't really want me to."

I force my face to remain expressionless. What in the world has dear Nathan, teenage-son-of-mine, gotten himself into *this* time?

"It's been so long since it all happened but I told him I was going to tell you. You need to know. Don't be mad at him. Okay? Promise?"

The fragrant coffee aroma does nothing to quiet the alarm bells going off in my head.

Afton taps my hand. "Promise?"

I shake my head. "Promise what? What did you say?"

"Promise not to be mad at Nathan … you know, after I tell you."

"It kind of depends on what you have to tell me, Afton."

"Honey," Afton's mom elbows her. "Mrs. G is probably very busy. Say what you need to say so she can be on her way."

Afton closes her eyes for a second then opens them. "Remember when … remember when I had the, you know, abortion?"

I clamp my lips shut.

Afton frowns. "Sorry. How can anyone forget that?"

The bell above the door jingles. I glance to see who's coming in.

Afton drags me back to the conversation with, "Before I decided to do it, Nathan and I talked, a lot."

I nod.

"And you know how everyone was all in my face about having a paternity test?"

"Stop it, Afton!" Her mom cuffs her on the shoulder. "Drop the drama."

Afton glares at her and then in unison, they face me with comic-almost-happy-face expressions.

What the hell am I doing here with these two lunatics?

I take a sip of coffee.

"When Nathan and I were talking, I told him something." Afton stops, inhales, then looks me straight in the eyes and says, "I told him it wasn't his baby."

My heart stops.

"It was Brian's. You know Brian? The guy that races dirt bikes." Afton does motorcycle driving hand motions. "He's a lot of fun but he's not ready to be a dad. He can't even take care of himself."

Afton's mom pinches Afton's arm hard enough to make her wince. "Quit it! I'm not going to tell you again."

I try to breathe but there's no air in the room.

"It wasn't Nathan's baby?" I whisper.

"No, no. It wasn't. That's what I'm trying to tell you. It was Brian's." She looks out the window for a second. "I knew he was not super responsible. Not like Nathan. I wanted the best for the baby. And I thought, no, I *knew* Nathan wouldn't let me down. So I told everyone it was his."

I can't blink. Or breathe.

"But I told Nathan before I … before I ended it so he would know. I didn't want him to be all bummed out."

"He never said a word," I shake my head ever so slightly. "He never told us."

"I know. He tried to. He wanted to. But everyone was so tense. He never found the right time. And then, when it was over, I never saw you guys."

I blink.

"I ran into Nathan last week and he said things were kind of back to normal at home. He didn't want to get you all," Afton raises quote fingers in the air and says, "'wound up' again."

"He knew," I stare into my coffee cup, "and he didn't tell me?"

"I know. I'm so sorry. That's why I wanted to tell you. Mom and I talked and she said it wasn't fair you didn't know. She figured you'd being going through all that gramma-guilt stuff. And being sad. I didn't want that. Not if I could help it. Life's too short."

"We all thought," I look up at her, "everyone in town thinks …"

"I know. I'm sorry about that too. There's a ton of stuff I screwed up." She shrugs. "But I can't fix it. Brian doesn't know. And there's no point telling him now. It's not like he can do anything about it. Besides, he'd go totally ballistic. He'd really lose it."

"*He'd* lose it?" I say.

Afton's mom sits up straight and presses her clasped hands into the edge of the table.

Air whistles out my nostrils.

"So, let me get this straight." I say slowly as I lift my left hand in front of me and spread my fingers out. "First, you tell Nathan you're pregnant with his baby after you guys had split up. For months." I bend down my index finger. "Then I take you to the clinic to confirm you're pregnant." Next finger bends. "When you wanted someone to go with you, I came along to the doctor appointments. We made sure both you and the baby were healthy." I look up at them as I push my ring finger against the others.

Afton and her mom frown and drop their eyes to my raised hand.

"And then, before you have the abor … you tell Nathan it's not his." I push my pinkie finger into the palm of my hand. My thumb is the only one standing. I poke it. "But no one tells me? We spend months agonizing over it. And no one has the decency to tell us?"

"I'm *so* sorry." Afton rubs my arms.

I flex my forearm.

"You know Nathan." She gives me a sugar-sweet smile. "He hates seeing people get into shit. He's the one always trying to fix stuff so everyone gets along. He didn't want you to not like me or think I'm this terrible person. He's such a great guy."

"Really?" I tap the side of my cup. "He's such a great guy?"

"Yeah. He would have been there for me, the whole way. I know that. You did an awesome job raising him."

I remain stone-faced. "You think so, do you?"

For a few seconds the coffee shop noises fill the quiet between the three of us.

"So, are we good?" Afton points to me then herself. "Are we good now? Everything's out. No more secrets."

I glance from her to her mom then back to her.

"I'm glad you know now." She claps her hands together. "I'm so glad I told you."

I take a deep breath, hold it and let it out in a steady exhale. Then I pick up my purse and my jacket. I stand up and reach over to shake Afton's mom's hand. Her watery eyes blink. She leans over, squeezes my hand and nods her head a few times. Afton jumps up and gives me a giant bear hug. She pushes back to look up at me but doesn't let go then pulls me in and hugs me hard again. I pat her back and rest my chin on her head.

My heels click on the tiles as I force my legs to walk to the door. I pass tables with people deep in conversation, some laughing, hand gestures in the air. My heart thumps so loud but no one looks up. I focus on the exit.

When I get into the car, I put on my seatbelt and take deep breaths. In. Out. In out. The seatbelt digs into my heart. This breathing exercise, it's supposed to keep me from flying off the handle. Sometimes it works. I breathe in and out eleven more times till my chest stops feeling like it will implode.

I drive home, conscious to keep my fingers light on the steering wheel. Once the car is parked in the driveway, my face gets warm. The steady pulse in my ear gets louder again.

***

"Nathan!" I slam the front door shut. "Get in here. Now!"

The basement door squeaks open.

"Hey, Mom." Nathan tips his head back. "What's going on?"

"Don't you dare 'Hey, Mom' me, Mister!"

He nods that slow nod that his dad does when he's trying to figure out what I'm pissed about.

I throw my purse on the chair. "How dare you!"

"Mom." Nathan head stops moving. "I love you."

I can't answer.

Judge's Comment

This story built up to its shattering moment of revelation with an unrelenting emotional tension. The story's success is not in any twist or surprise, but in the momentum that the author builds in the main character. A deeply affecting story.

About Barbara Wackerle Baker

Barbara Wackerle Baker grew up in Banff, Alberta, and spends her free time racing up and down the Rockies to keep up with an active family of outdoor enthusiasts. Her passions include: writing, photography, exploring landscapes, and time with her grandchildren (the most beautiful grandchildren ever). Three of her stories have found homes in *Chicken Soup* publications, one is included in *Prairie Fire*'s 2017 Spring Anthology, a dozen others are in short story contest anthologies and she was awarded the John Kenneth Galbraith Short Fiction award in 2016.

Night Swim
by Di Golding

Right away this trip felt different, except for the dull headache I always got when we flew in the smoking section. When I complained, Mum blamed the six packets of sugar I made the stewardess put in my grapefruit juice, then she dropped her carry-on at the taxi stand. Usually we'd be greeted by Louie in his burnt orange Cadillac Coupe De Ville. My older brothers would shove our luggage into the cavernous trunk, and Louie would pick me up and say, "How's my Raggedy Ann?" Instead, Mum, my brother Reid, and I crowded into the back of a Plymouth that smelled like feet.

Mum smiled and said, "Pinellas Park, please and thank you!" In the rearview mirror I watched her face fall as the cabbie steered out of the lineup. In the last few months she'd adopted a mask that she thought I couldn't see. She still smiled, she still laughed. She still went curling on Saturdays. But there was no joy. She'd stay like that for a couple of years. Eventually the joy would return, but I didn't know it then.

Dad had never made the trip with us to visit Grandmother and Louie in Florida. He said he hated flying. Really, he and Louie never managed more than a cursory respect for one another. "No man is good enough for your daughter," Dad would say after a long draw from his third or fourth bottle of Export "you'll understand some day." But I understood then. I was smarter at eleven than I am now.

"Grandmother isn't having an easy go," Mum warned as we pulled onto the freeway, "she's not herself." But when we arrived Grandmother was waiting for us on her screened-in porch, and she skipped over to hug me, all smiles. Real smiles. She smelled like Rose Milk and when she cupped my face in her hands her nails were still perfect. In the carport Louie's Cadillac was cloudy with a fine dust. The car hadn't moved since the previous September and Mum was worried that it might not start without a boost. My oldest brother Dean was driving down from Ottawa with his scandalously older girlfriend Mandy. They were bringing Mandy's daughter Robyn, who was fourteen and had massive boobs already. They were due to arrive the following day and Mum was going to let Dean deal with the Caddie.

This trip wasn't supposed to be fun. Mum was here to see to Grandmother's affairs because Louie had always done everything. Grandmother didn't even have a driver's license. Mum had vowed at a young age that she would never live like that. She ran our household. Each Friday until he got too sick to work, Dad would hand Mum his pay packet from Canadian International Paper and she'd dole out his allowance. When Dad died in February I felt guilty because I knew that if I'd had to choose one parent to die it would have been him. I didn't love him less, but he just would have been a shambles in a situation like this.

As usual I was the only kid at the Pinellas Park seniors' complex. I had to wear a swim cap in the pool and I wasn't allowed to splash or dive. Reid was nineteen, and he didn't want to play how-long-can-you-hold-your-breath-underwater with me anymore. He reclined on a lounger and read *Basketball Digest* beside residents with skin brown, and wrinkled like jerky. They stage whispered to one another on the pool deck; "Those are Annie's grandkids. They lost their grandfather, then their father. Boom, boom. Just like that. *Cancer.*"

When Robyn arrived the next day, all she wanted to do was listen to her Walkman and work on her tan. She'd go on to a career in finance and live in places like Milan and Singapore and Tokyo, but she was already too cool for this pool. The residents clucked tongues at her racy, zip-up Body Glove swim-suit and sickly-sweet coconut Coppertone spray, but she couldn't hear them, and if she did she didn't care. I heard a bi-plane overhead and I squinted up to see it pulling a sign: 'Senor Froggy's — 2 for 1 Margaritas". Shade hit me abruptly. It was Dean towering over me from the edge of the pool. "Get ready", he barked, "we're going to the beach."

I sat cross-legged on the hump in the back seat of the Caddie between Robyn, who snapped her Hubba-Bubba like it was the most boring thing in the world, and Mandy who smoked and pretended not to notice as her flicked ashes drifted back into the car. Dean drove and scolded Reid for not folding the map properly. I looked out the window and saw the IHOP where Louie used to take us to for silver dollar pancakes. Dean turned up the radio when it played Dire Straits and sang along. "I waaaant my MTVeeee!". We passed malls, and shopping plazas with stores we didn't have in Canada: J.C. Penny, Macys, Nordstrom. Billboards for Oakley and Pepsi and even Sea World were American and sexy and new.

Dean had wanted to be at the beach earlier but the Caddie was stubborn to start. By the time we arrived most people were packing up. Mandy and Robyn placed their straw beach mats to face the waning sun. I dropped my towel and threw off my cover-up in one swift motion and ran for the water. "Only Canadians swim in the ocean in winter", I could hear Louie say. It was cold and my toes turned blue but I splashed in farther. Long, slippery sea oats slithered around my ankles like slimy ghost hands, and they gave me the willies so I pushed out deeper. I'd recently become an expert at acting like nothing scared me.

    I made it to a sandbar and launched myself up into each wave, struggling to ride it before it crested. I did this until my eyes burned from the salt and my legs ached from kicking. I saw my family on the shore. They were eating cold fried chicken and passing around a jumbo bag of Utz potato chips. They didn't see me. I'd been in the water so long I'd become invisible. The sun began its slow melt into the ocean. The waves turned orange at the edges like the Polaroids in our photo album at home. I floated on my back and watched the daylight disappear.

    I didn't see the fin right away. It cut swiftly through the water a few metres from me. I planted my feet on the soft sand and froze. I looked toward the beach and saw two adults near the shore tinkering with a big metal box. One of them, a young, tanned woman, waved at me and called out, "It's okay, they're friendly. Put out your hand." I stretched my arm out, palm down and waited. I saw a deep, black, marble eye focused on me. Its body slid beneath my hand like thick, smooth rubber. I shivered. I stayed. We played this game, the two dolphins and I; me reaching out, my hands sliding over and over until my arms trembled.

    I don't remember coming out of the water. I don't remember the ride home, past the J.C Penny, the IHOP or the billboards. I don't remember the rest of the trip, the cab ride back to the airport, the smoke-filled cabin, or the drive back to our cluttered, snow-covered house in Hawkesbury. But it must have happened.

I remember everything else. I remember years later when I had to carry Grandmother from her bedroom in Mum's house to the bathroom, and laying her in the warm tub, her eyes wet and wide, scared because she no longer knew me. Years after that Mum lay dying in a hospital bed in my living room. I rubbed lotion on her dry, atrophied legs and bits of her white skin fell on my hand like snowflakes. I told myself: *Don't forget this. Don't forget this.*

Last winter, after Mum had passed, I went skating on the Rideau Canal with Robyn. Mandy and Dean had long since broken up but we'd remained friendly. We stopped at a shack so Robyn could buy her teenaged daughter a hot chocolate. I asked Robyn if she remembered our trip to Florida. "Vaguely," she offered, "why?" I asked her if she remembered that I swam with dolphins. I described every bit of that day, down to the colour of the dolphin lady's t-shirt. Robyn looked at me bemusedly and snorted. "*That* didn't happen."

Once, in the car on the way to one of Mum's cancer treatments she grinned at me proudly and said, "You've always been strong, especially after your father died." I turned to look at her and said, "The childhood I had, and the childhood *you think* I had were two very different things." Her grin collapsed and she said, "Of course they were. They should be. Honestly, I don't remember much right after your father died. The mind does incredible things to cope, to keep you alive and breathing and upright. I know I was strong, and you were strong, but don't ask me for details"

Walking home from the Canal I breathed, I stood upright. I looked at faces. I wondered which ones were real, and which were masks. I wondered who was going through the hardest moment of their life right now. Who had been to hell and back and could I see it. What were the details? How many of these faces will cry tears in the shower at home, or in their car during lunch break? Will their kids see it and pretend they didn't? I thought about all the eleven year olds swimming with dolphins. I could smell the brine of the water, feel the sticky salt on skin. If that isn't real, than neither is anything before or after.

Judge's Comment
The rich details in this story set up an emotional impact that hinges on memory, and leaves the reader almost desolate in sympathy for the main character's losses. We're left to question what's real, and to decide whether to despair or hope because of our answer. This story hits hard, and leaves a mark.

About Di Golding
Di Golding is an Ottawa-based film critic and editor for dearcastandcrew.com, She is a regular contributor to *Ottawa Magazine*, and is a replacement film reviewer for LiVE 88.5 FM. Di is also a freelance on-air contributor for CBC Radio Ottawa's *All In A Day* programme, and a freelance on-air contributor for CBC Radio Canada. She studied scriptwriting at Algonquin College, and studied comedy screenwriting under *SCTV* scribe Dave Flaherty through Humber College. Di has what psychiatrists and her husband would describe as an "unhealthy obsession" with Jeff Bridges. She also has exactly one IMDb credit.

Distant Connections
by Julio Heleno Gomes

The wooden door creaks open and the room is shrouded in gloom but for dusty streaks breaking through the slats of the shutters. A tang of liniment and sweat hangs in the air. A small bed is jammed at the far wall, a pierced Jesus looking down. Under a tattered quilt lies my dying grandmother.

"Come in. Don't make too much noise," my aunt commands, ushering us into the musty room.

My father, never at ease in situations that require displays of affection, steps in uncertainly. My mother shepherds my siblings as if they're about to view a freak show exhibit, which it could be with our Avó, a shrunken figure stretched formlessly under the covers, grey hair sprayed across a stained pillow, a bird-like hand resting on a frayed edge of the quilt,. She seemed as near to death as life.

We gather round the low bed, my father staring at the mother he hasn't seen in years. My mother's hands rest on the shoulders of Sara, who looks on in discomfort, and Carlitos, who glances curiously around the spartan room, reflexively sticking a thumb in his mouth though he long outgrew the habit. I lurk behind my mother as my aunt shuffles along the gap between the bed and the plaster wall, reaching to open the shutters over the bed.

"*Ela não se sentindo bem,*" she informs us, unnecessarily, in Portuguese, that her mother hasn't been feeling well. "*Mãe,*" she grunts, leaning in to shake her by the shoulder. "*Mãe!*"

My mother scowls at my unheeding father, then moves forward and gently takes the bony hand clutching the quilt and strokes it.

"Natividade," she whispers, running a hand over my grandmother's shadowed face.

She finally turns to us, eyes shining behind fluttering lids. She trembles and a dry cough racks her body. Her fingers snatch at my mother's wrist.

"*Está tudo aqui,*" Avó sputters between coughs, wearily looking about. "*Eu sabia.*"

Yes, she knew we would come, all of us. What else could we do when the unusual phone call came, saying Mother's been sick for a while now, very sick, and this time the end is surely near, she is being summoned to her Saviour. Such words when relayed to we the children in far-off Canada rang oddly. Avó never struck me as the religious type despite the Jesus statue over the bed or a name that evoked Christmas cheer and the love of the Virgin Mary. Our visits to the old country I remembered as awkward encounters with Natividade, though my mother would tell us that our departing would result in a barrage of lament. "Oh, me," Avó would weep to my father, in bitterness and recrimination, "I'll never see you or these precious children again. They'll forget about me just as you have forgotten about us." Funny, such emotion from a woman who gave affection as easily as she handed out coins for the grandkids to buy candy. Which is to say, not much.

So the trip back home, undertaken in haste this time, looked likely to settle into a grim countdown to last rites for the old lady.

"What is the matter with her?" Sara said with a sour turn of her mouth after we were shooed away from the cramped room so father could spend quiet time with his mother, who we were informed by my aunt may not make it another day.

"It's her heart, dear," my mother said soothingly, taking Carlitos by the hand.

"What heart problem? She's probably got pneumonia," I said. "Or is it bronchitis? Emphysema? Sounds like no one knows."

"Antonio, she have the problems with 'er heart. For many years now," my mother replied, irked by something more than the scepticism of unsympathetic teenagers.

"How come she's not in the hospital?" my sister persisted.

"Doctors do nothing," my mother replied, her halting English faltering. "Too much *antibioticos*. She have the chest problem now, she be old seventy years and not young woman. Be nice to your Avó."

Sara and I exchanged knowing glances. We'd heard this before and knew what it meant. A vigil for the three weeks we were booked to be here, trooping in every day to pay our respects to the old woman, now a bundle of brittle bones lying in the grim room at the back reserved for the unwanted and the unwell, where her own husband had been banished years ago when cancer started to eat away his life.

The gaggle of cousins next door offered a break from the tedium. The boys and I would trudge up to the sandy soccer field and boot a ragged ball around or we'd race from the school building back to our house, the winner promised a swig from the bottles of Wiser's De Luxe my father had brought to share with his brother. Invariably I would win but would decline the prize. I preferred *sumol*, the orange fruit drink, so the cousins would gleefully help themselves to the whiskey bottle.

My siblings cavorted with the girls, dashing through the crumbling barn and hay shed, chasing chicks and alarmed hens around the straw-covered courtyard or pulling tabbies out from under the crooked stools where they had been curled up, brushing their backs in careless strokes. Then my aunt would emerge from the main house, drying her rough hands on the ever-present apron (she had a dozen of them and they were every shade of black), and bark at one of her daughters to go and check on Avó, who in turn would grumble and direct another sibling to go, a routine which concluded with the youngest trampling hesitantly into the old house to make sure grandmother was still in this world.

At least once on the trip my father would get itchy feet and rent an exotic car and in his shilly-shally shifting would send us hurtling along twisting, oak-fringed roads, stopping at sacred springs, untended shrines and obscure chapels so my mother could kneel reverently before dim altars, sighing Ave Marias and Our Fathers, beseeching Jesus, as well as the apostles and all the saints, to bless poor Natividade and release her from her earthly suffering.

"Tozé," my mother said one evening as she carried platters of barbecued chicken and roasted potatoes to the dinner table, using my pet name. "I promise your Avó I make *caldo verde* for her. It be 'er favourite. You take to her some? Your *tia* said this be good time she eat."

I rolled my eyes. Knowing a protest would be pointless I took the bowl and trudged next door. I nudged my way through the high metal gates into the silent courtyard and entered the old house, past the soot-blackened old kitchen, and into the sick room.

"*Avó, caldo verde. É para você,*" I said as I entered, presenting the bowl as if a peace offering.

She was sitting up and looked at me, unmoving, like a wax figure. I sighed, took the cloth and tucked it under her chin, stirred the potato purée and shredded cabbage soup and began feeding her small portions. After a half-dozen spoonfuls, she shook her head and said, "*Não quero mais.*" That was enough.

I put the spoon down, took the cloth and dabbed her lips, then lifted a cup of water from which she sipped before slowly shifting back into the pillows, still crumpled and stained.

Well, I've done my good grandson deed, I thought. I grabbed the bowl, collected the spoon and turned without a word or backward glance.

"Antonio José," I heard.

It came as a hacking croak but it was a definite address. On the few occasions she spoke directly to me, she was deliberate in using the names that had been entered in the parish registry, the only one, besides my aunt, who persisted with that formality.

"Did I ever tell you," she said in a low but steady voice, "about me and your grandfather?"

I didn't know what she meant since I knew so very little of their life. "*Não,*" I said with no interest.

She turned her head to indicate a cane chair behind the door. I put the bowl and spoon on the bedside table, went to the chair, carried it up to the bed and sat, my hands folded in my lap, waiting. I watched the dust motes dance as the faint sunlight flickered through the shutters.

She wasn't from these parts, you understand. She grew up a ways away in a fishing village east of the capital (which I think explains the singsong enunciation in her syllables). Her father was *um pescador*, her mother a fishmonger's wife. The bounty of the sea was all they knew, both the fish from the deep and from the rocky waters past the harbour, the waters that glided up the beach, the beach of the softest sand, where up would go a magnificent hotel, to stand like a palace over the bay. It was here as a young woman, still almost a child, she broke from the tradition of her family and went to work as a maid, changing bedsheets, dusting and sweeping rooms occupied by foreign nobles and the Americans who became rich from that great war. But she still had chores each morning at the dock helping her mother sort the catch her father had taken into his dory. It was a sturdy twenty-footer that would go beyond the horizon and the safety of the coast, in every kind of weather, bringing back baskets filled with haddock, hake, tuna and occasionally — oh, what a treat! — octopus or red lobster. She had two older brothers and they had their own fine *barco*, but it could not compare with father's. One morning she went to meet her father's boat and along with Senhor Rodrigo there was someone else on board. A young man with a thin curl of a moustache like the movie star, not Valentino or Gable but William Powell, and his eyes would sparkle when he told a story, which tended to be amusing though sometimes it was crude, told in no hurry as he tapped tobacco from a small pouch and into the white paper, pausing to roll it and run his tongue along the edge before putting it between his lips and striking a match. He was José, come from the land of the great pine forests, looking to make a mark in the City of Light, at the mouth of the mighty river, as those sad songs tell us, from whence great adventurers set out on their voyages of discovery all those years ago, bidding *adeus* to stone-faced mothers and fearful brides. Of ocean fishing José knew very little and clearly it was not suited to his temperament or ambition. It was only because of the unsurpassed beauty of Captain Antonio's daughter that he endured the early morning sailings, the bitter winds, and the calluses and sore muscles the heavy oars and seaweed-soaked nets produced. I will walk through fire for you, he once said — that and many other sweet words when he came by the modest house to share in the meal of *sardinhas* her mother would grill in the afternoon along with her special cornmeal bread, drinking the *vinho verde* brought by Senhor Rodrigo.

Natividade, the only daughter and so it must be her father's favourite child and her mother's constant companion, deserved better than the adoration of *un vagabundo* from the north who was so lacking in talent he had to sign on for the muscle-straining, soul-sapping monotony of trolling the waves for profit, as her mother would comment while they sat by the open fire knitting the caps, shawls and sweaters to sell at the monthly fair. Better to stay at that castle on the beach and clean the chamber pots of those who are so rich you are like the furniture to them, though one to whom they might leave the occasional *réis* as thanks for a job well done, she advised quietly, for her mother was a woman of great piety and only raised her voice when competing at the fish market.

Life on the deep waters is, *é verdade*, humdrum and hard work. You must have a keen eye to the danger that can come like the wolf from distant clouds and the gathering breeze. So it was one November morning as the boat was out beyond the cape that a storm arose before the sun had properly kissed the cliffs. An old hand on these sometimes impetuous seas, her father was still caught out by the suddenness of the storm. His brute strength and guile was not enough against the fury of that mad wind, the waves it inspired, and the freezing rain. They struggled like brave Odysseus to turn for home but the boat was swamped, the boom of the sail broken like a dry branch, the oars plucked from their hands. A swell of clashing waves turned them sideways and smashed the boat on the rocks. Father and Senhor Rodrigo were taken by the merciless water. José ended up on a large outcropping, a wicker fishing basket held tightly to his chest, shivering in cold and fear, one arm broken and his skin scraped from bootless foot to head. He was found at dusk by her brothers, the only thing that was saved from that storm. And when a respectable period of mourning had passed he vowed never to step off solid ground and that he was done with this village and the meagre life of fishing. What future did a heartbroken Natividade have but to accept his offer of marriage and leave her world behind for a future that if it would not be better could not be worse?

"Do you understand?" she asked me weakly.

"Yes," I said gravelly and we looked at each other, saying nothing but much passing between us.

It would transpire that tragedy would not be a thing in their past. Their first children were twin boys, such a unique event it was hailed as a blessing. They were christened Antonio and José. They died in infancy, of scarlet fever, when a sick Natividade was breast feeding. The mantle was passed on to me, my mother would explain years later, the first of all the grandchildren and named in this fashion so my father might get out from under the shadow that hung over his father and the two boys and two girls that followed, a gift to his mother that seemed never to have been accepted. But I now know that like the ghost of her long lost father that too has at last been laid to rest.

Judge's Comment
Each of the senses is alive when reading this richly descriptive story. The imagery is only a backdrop, though, for the heavy threads of history, loss, and absence. But the distinctly and naturally drawn characters engage the reader closely with the family and its problematic past.

About Julio Heleno Gomes
Julio Heleno Gomes was born in a small village in Portugal and came as a youngster with his mother and sister to join their father in a new life in Canada. He's a long-time resident of Thunder Bay and has worked in journalism for more than 25 years, where he was able to combine his passion for daily reportage with flights into fiction writing. Along with a love of reading, Julio also enjoys music, film and sports.

Winners and Honourable Mentions of Previous Years

Through great effort on the part of several stalwart "detectives" we were able to track down the names of previous winners and honourable mentions from 1992 to 1997 and from 2005 to last year's 2016. Pre-computer-age paper trails fade away as does contact information.

If this Anthology gets into the hands of anyone with the missing information for 1986–1991 and 1998–2004, please contact Canadian Authors Association–National Capital Region branch and we'll revise this edition.

Thank you.

1992

Structured poem

Kevin Regalbuto

Russell Smith

Barbara Benson

Free Verse

Sylvia Adams

Leslie Smith Dow

Ellen Drennan

Honourable Mention

Sylvia Adams

Smith Dow

Ronnie Brown

Helen Rodney

Haiku

A.N. Coram

Agnes Bright

Kathleen Hovey

Honourable Mention

Ronnie Brown

Brian Yamaskika

A. Coram

1993

Article

Eleanor McSheffrey

Belinda Dunn

Tom MacGregor

Short Story

R.K. Webb

William Ritchford

Eleanor McSheffrey

Juvenile Short Story

Karleen Bradford

Ben Scheer

Karleen Bradford

1994

Structured Poem

Catherine Walsh (three)

Short Free Verse

Sylvia Adams

David Henderson

Ellen Drennan

Haiku

Gill Foss

Ronnie Brown

1995

Short Story

Linda Lord

Sylvia Adams

Karen Massey

Article

Sylvia Adams

Colin Leys

Peggy de Jourdan

Juvenile Short Story

Brian Doyle

Linda Kennedy

Marjorie Robertson

1996

Structured Poem

Norma Rae

Russell Smith

Eileen Robinson

Haiku

Ronnie Brown

J.H. Mann

Debbie Walker

Short Free Verse

Jeff Bien

Joanne John

J. Buschek

1997

Adult Fiction

J.Y. Hewitt

J.H. Mann

Stephen J. Fischer

Juvenile Fiction

J.H. Mann

Betty Warrington-Kearsley

Margaret Bunel Edwards

Non- fiction

Paul Mackan

Beatrice Biederman

Frederick A. Walker

2005

Article

1st Place Betty Warrington-Kearsley
"A Walk Down the Old Road"

3rd Place Betty Nygaard King

Short Story

1st Place Gertrud Baer
"The Puzzle Piece"

Poetry

Honourable Mention

Ruth Latta (two)

Young Adult

1st Place Bushra Khan

2nd Place Taha Hassan

2006
Children's Literature

Judged by Shirley Byers

Shirley Byers is a contributing editor for *WITH* magazine, a U.S. teen publication, and she has also been published in *Highlights for Children, Listen, Brio* and others. Her short story "Lightening up Jackie" was included in the anthology *Best of the Children's Market* published by the Institute of Children's Literature in 2000 and her book, *Cat and Mom Story*, was published by Scholastic in 1989. She lives in Saskatchewan.

1st Place Margaret Smith
"Katy and the Almost-Neglected Kitten:

"Divorce stories have been done before but this writer gave it a new twist and handled it beautifully. I can see this story as a picture book. The protagonist would probably have to be a little younger but that wouldn't detract from the story. In a few adept brush strokes you have given us Katy. The reader sees and knows this little girl and empathizes with her. The cat/kitten conversation between Katy and her grandfather is an excellent example of 'show don't tell.' Without glossing over reality the story offers an explanation and hope to children in similar circumstances. Good job!"

2nd Place Sharon Rudnitski
"Wauna's Song"

"From a great beginning that draws the reader in to a resolution that satisfies, this was a terrific story. My only problem with this story was the rather cliché 'You achieve what you believe,' offered up by Wiscasa. Good use of word pictures and bits of humour provided a nice touch. Without being preachy, you handled well Wauna's decision to sacrifice her own 'cool' in order to thaw the Snow Woman."

3rd Place Gail Gernat
"And Matthew Was a Dinosaur"

"This is a lovely, well-told tale which does a good job of combining humour and sentiment. Good use of repetition which works well in children's stories. I loved your kid-friendly word pictures such as Matthew spent all night walking around and looking at things from on top."

Poetry

Judged by Catherine McVicar,

Catherine McVicar is co-author of the Peterborough Prose Group's *Murder at Market Hall*. She writes poetry, short stories and children's stories. Her children's fantasy novel, *The Grass beyond the Door*, was published by Methuen (UK) in 1978. Since then she has had works published in magazines and in small press anthologies.

1st Place Holly Kritsch
"Almost like Love"

"The poet makes every word count in this spare and elegant poem. The poignant result touches the reader's heart."

2nd Place J. S. Tannahill
"The Science Not Taught"
"The poet light-heartedly connects the sensual and the intellectual; the reader smiles throughout at this pleasing conceit."

3rd Place Wendy Moore "Balance"
"This is a lovely prose poem containing images that are vivid, satisfying and memorable."

Short Story

Judged by Claire Sullivan

"Claire Sullivan is Past President of CAA's Peterborough Branch and Co-Chair of the CanWrite! Conference 2007 committee. She co-wrote three chapters of the Peterborough Prose Group's Murder at Market Hall, is a regular contributor to Grainews, and is currently working on her second novel."

1st Place Ken McBeath
"My Old Man"
"Slightly wordy in some places. This story has intrigue, pathos and emotion. Congratulations!"

2nd Place Patrick Fitzgerald "A Fine and Private Place"
"Good foreshadowing, use of senses, language, details. An engaging story. Congratulations!"

3rd Place Radhika Sekar
"An Un-arranged Marriage"

"I enjoyed the humour of this story and learned about a culture I wasn't familiar with. Suggestion: Let the dialogue speak for itself, rather than using descriptive (distracting) tags; e.g., "she pleaded", "wailed Sweeta", "shrugged Anu," etc. He said, she said is less intrusive. Well written. Good dialogue, tension, descriptions, and foreshadowing. Interesting plot. Congratulations!"

Non-Fiction/Creative Non-Fiction

Judged by Joan Eyolfson Cadham

Joan Eyolfson Cadham is an award-winning freelance writer/editor/photographer and a practising storyteller of Icelandic fairy tales. She's had two books published by Shoreline Press and has another two books in the works. Joan lives in Foam Lake, Saskatchewan and is currently the National President of the Canadian Authors Association.

Judge's Comments

"Because this was non-fiction/creative non-fiction, I was looking for something that would sell, a piece of writing that was marketable without major rewriting, although perhaps with some final editing and tightening.

"I wanted an opening sentence that would propel me toward the second, and the next — sentences that sang — and powerful or quixotic word pictures. If there was humour, I wanted it to be natural, part of the story line, not forced, or that contributed.

"I was looking, most particularly, for strict attention to the act of showing. The theme had to be memorable — but so did the telling.

"I wanted something that wasn't just a personal recollection. I was looking for a private event with a universal message, and evidence that the author is changed at the end of the piece in ways he or she is only beginning to recognize, and that the change is more than one-dimensional.

"As a result, in the winning pieces, I cared that the insight had happened."

1st Place Anne Kathleen McLaughlin
"Waking Up in Oregon"

2nd Place Michael Grier
"Walk"

3rd Place Jennifer Haney
"Missing Pages"

2007
Poetry

Judged by Sheila Martindale, Victoria, British Columbia

1st Place Ronnie R. Brown
"News Photo 1"

"This is a very insightful poem — the writer is able to put himself/herself in another person's shoes and know how she feels. There is also a wonderful comparison between the death and destruction we see and hear about every day, and how the death of one person can affect us. It is a marvellous narrative poem, without being in any way prosaic. The language is straightforward and conversational, without sacrificing lyricism."

2nd Place Margaret Malloch Zielinski "Remembering Christmas"

"This poem puts the reader right in the picture, in England in the middle of the last century. The pantomime comes alive, we can feel the exhilaration of tobogganing during a rare snowfall. And the gypsies! Very real. Again, accessible language with the music very much there."

3rd Place Rosalie Adams
"Alzheimer's"

"We can feel the pain of this person, whose life has been robbed by this terrible condition. Reading this poem made me feel as if I were in a bad dream, where nothing made any sense and where I was lost, never to be found. Extremely moving and well-written."

Honourable Mention

Gill Foss
"Canoe at Sunset"

"A beautiful descriptive poem, with some lively assonance and semi-rhymes. It paints a picture, which we can see with great clarity, and the words are lovely and unpretentious."

Ken McBeath
"Sentry Duty, Africa"

"The nervousness of the new sentry duty guard is palpable, and we feel his fear of the known and the unknown. The alternating long and short lines are very effective. Like a good mystery story, it has the reader on the edge of his/her seat."

Sarah Perry
"I Still Dream of Rosseau"

"What a beautiful piece of nostalgia! This writer is not going to let reality spoil his/her memories of summer spent at Grandma's, when the world was a different place, childhood was charmed, and everything was free but also safe. A delightful poem."

Short Story

1st Place Arlene Smith
"Ruby Slippers"

"I immediately felt that 'Ruby Slippers' was crafted by the hands of an experienced writer. The masterful juxtaposition of the two worlds colliding between father and son pulled me into the story with ease. The blend of scenes and moods impressed from start to finish. Particularly enjoyed that it really boiled down to an age-old story of father and son attempting to find common ground even though they appeared to be so different."

2nd Place Charles Hubbard
"Three Cardboard Boxes"

"This story appeals to my personal tastes. It reminds me of the classic stories of early science fiction that appeared in magazines and were then collected for generations to read. It also contains all the aspects of story writing that I teach my own students. Read it once for enjoyment then read it again to see how it is crafted."

3rd Place Ken McBeath
"Damsel with a Dulcimer"

"A love story of sorts. Also a mystery/thriller on the edge of horror at times. A joyous blend of conflict and resolution that doesn't suit the lives of all characters but still brings people together in the end. All characters have such distinctly different purposes within a tightly written circumstance. Manages to make the reader feel an entire rainbow of emotions."

Honourable Mention

Ramma Kamra
"Quenching the Thirst"

"Writer selected powerful moments of history and demonstrated why they are so relevant today. Also demonstrated how such different worlds can be pulled together when the correct trigger is in place. The pain is felt in moments that surge through your veins as you read."

Phil Caron
"A Practical Man"

"Ah, the burden of responsibility. People live some incredible lives — or perhaps incredibly ordinary lives — as a result of that weight. This story captures the feelings that can span the decades and then catch us so unaware. Sometimes it takes our children to teach us what next step to take."

Kristine Swaren
"It Must Have Been the Sawdust"

"A touching story that doesn't get too sentimental. Feminine point of view is handled with humour and skill. Curious whether a man pulled this off or if only a woman can write this way. Great fun to watch the fumblings and recoveries under the watchful eye of the narrator. Happy endings can be such fun when handled so well."

2008

Poetry

Judged by Bernice Lever

1st Place Christy Cochrane
"One Oak"

"Displaying fresh, rich images that push the readers and listeners to consider oak trees, any trees, anew is the first prize poem. Good poetry, which 'One Oak' is, reaches both one's heart and head. It is a delight to one's tongue and ear to read aloud this poem with its good rhymes and alliteration. Its final line sends one back to its opening stanzas to reread, to re-imagine these unique word pictures. It is a poem others will quote in awe for its strong narrative filled with surprising metaphors."

2nd Place Marcia Taylor
"Autistic"

"Using a finely controlled form of set rhymes with only room for a few images allowed, this poet creates a powerful message about its subject. 'Autistic' teaches readers to see this child as a needed gift, not as a subject to pity or to avoid. Poetic forms can be used for comical, even easy lines, but this poet writes a terza rima form excellently and memorably."

3rd Place Lise M. Rochefort
"Even though You're Dead"

"This is a grand example of a prose type poem recounting an anecdote in good cadence, even using dialogue lines. This poet's specific images draw the reader into not only the emotions of loss, but also wry acceptance. The contrasts of 'canal workers' and lawyers, the then and now, allow readers to experience sorrow that is softened by memories and humorous projections."

Honourable Mention

Lise M. Rochefort
"He was a Big Man"

"Surprising images explain one's conceding to the demands of a bully — whether in the bedroom or the boardroom. The 'torn silk of fear' is interesting as silk is both a strong and beautiful fabric. That final line draws one back to the poem's beginning: 'my silence' and 'I needed him'. Strong poems, like this one, keep readers encircled with words."

Carol A. Stephen
"Tea Leaves"

"Here is a well-constructed poem with the word 'leaves' as both a noun and a verb. It is superbly aligned on the page for an effective reading. It is a beautifully understated poem about painful relationships that are so shredded that only over-used tea bags remain, instead of a once vitalizing love. There will be no more shared tea times, as this poem proves that often fewer words are more powerful messages than many words."

Gabriel Wainio-Theberge
"Winter"

"This poet employs the old symbolic contrasts of 'white/black' with amazing new insights from images of 'snow, ants and black' holes of space. 'Winter', with its demanding opinions, are posted for the reader to resolve. I also enjoyed the metaphorical images of 'cold' with its economy of words. This poet helps keep our language vital."

Short Story

Judged by Fred Kerner
(editorial director of Harlequin's North American operations)

1st Place Tesni Ellis
"Better Together"

"A touching yarn, beautifully told, and tear-inducing."

2nd Place Wayne Ng
"Julian's Feast"

"An unusual plot, well structured and carefully carried to its unexpected conclusion."

3rd Place Beverley Ann Colpitts
"A bolt from the Blue"

"A lovely, romantic tale that many newcomers to countless cities will recognize and sympathize with."

Honourable Mention

Mary Hagey
"The Wee Hours"

Ruth Latta
"God Spelled Backwards"

Anne Kathleen McLaughlin
"The Veiled Virgin"

Essay

Judged by Matt Bin, Oakville, Ontaro

1st Place Ruth Latta
"Prolific"

"A model of a good personal essay, the author takes a personal perspective and applies it more universally. The author gives the reader new insight into the writer's life with great interest and authority. A well-reasoned and well-researched essay that is food for thought for any serious writer in Canada. I finished the essay better informed, with new ideas, and with a desire to discuss the subject further with the author — the sign, I think, of a very successful essay."

2nd Place Roy Thomas
"The Poetry Proposal"

"A persuasive plea to include poetry in the humanitarian effort in Afghanistan, which should be of great interest to any Canadian. The author educates the reader about Afghan culture, and provides a clear plan for improving the cultural situation for women there."

3rd Place Krista Ranacher
"Water is Life"

"A fascinating account of life in Tanzania. The author's personal experiences bring a distant culture into immediate focus, and help to bridge the gap between our privileged lifestyle in Canada and the lack of life's most basic necessities in other parts of the world."

Honourable Mention

Derek North
"An Essay on the Merits of Planning Your Own Demise"

"A lively and creative approach to the morbid subject matter. I was not convinced to take the author's advice, but I appreciated his or her attempt."

Jon Peirce
"On Spell-Checkers"

"The author confronts a very common writers' tool and emerges, I think, with at least a draw. Any writer will appreciate the author's efforts to tame the perversities of computer spell-checking."

Iris Winston
"Pencil Thin and Other Fashions"

"Rumination on body image in the last few decades that makes a highly personal and emotional subject engaging and sympathetic in a most enjoyable essay."

Youth Short Story

Judged by Rhonda Stephenson

1st Place Alanna Ferguson
"The Most Complicated Puzzle"

"Highly imaginative, original work. Generally, good writing. Your over-the-top and out-of-the-box style coupled with unusual descriptions; i.e., 'relentless calm', create excellent humorous imagery. Good pace of action and dialogue.

"Additional information to help make your piece stronger: Intro a bit verbose and over-exaggerated. Tighten and capitalize by selecting key, potent words. Watch over-use of inverted phrases. These can be difficult to read, although they do serve as an asset to solid comedy writing. Be mindful of run-on sentences and repetition. Write lullabies as they sound. Social justice is a thoughtful and meaningful wrap-up which would be stronger if you chose to end with a statement versus a question. The puzzle should be solved unless this is a chapter for a manuscript."

2nd Place Samantha Morin
"Turning Point"

"A great read — a real page-turner with mature insight and self-reflection. Extremely moving tale. Very strong character profiles, definitely relational to the majority. Excellent depiction of typical sibling rivalry. Great rising action sustains intensity, depth and strength of story. Generally, good writing with functional dialogue.

"Additional information to help make your piece stronger: Watch consistency of tenses and asides; i.e., internal dialogue that is not necessary to development of storyline. This well-executed and clearly written storyline might be further enriched by embracing a more-diverse vocabulary. Just a few grammatical errors and punctuation mistakes."

3rd Place Gabriel Wainio-Theberge
"Crowsong"

"You are a true poet and storyteller! The opening draws the reader in by foreshadowing the explanation of nature's most provocative mysteries. Lovely passages of legendary folklore told with grace and wisdom. Beautiful descriptions of death and disparity. Nice attention to detail as we travel back in time through wonderful settings. Interesting turns of phrase, and fascinating imagery. Good use of dialogue and other technical elements of story structure. Super insight; poignant and relevant message. Fantastic concluding statement!

"Additional information to help make your piece stronger: Be mindful of separation of new ideas by beginning new paragraphs, and avoid introducing a new idea unless you plan to explore it. Watch over-use of certain verbs and run-on sentences. This can drag the story down and make it heavy for the reader at times."

Honourable Mention

Cameron R. H. Chown
"Partner"

Samantha Chown
No relation to Cameron
"Layla's Garden"

2009

Poetry

Judged by Harold Reinisch, Campbell River BC

1st Place Claudia Coutu Radmore,
Carleton Place
"Wild Thing Desiree"
"A Neophobic Tedium"
"She Walks in Beauty"

2nd Place Robert Sibley, Ottawa
"The Cedars at Point-no-Point"
"Old Soldier in his Garden"
"Ghirlandaio's Old Man and his Grandson"

3rd Place Gerry Murphy, Prescott
"December 21"
"Birch Grove"
"Winter"

Honourable Mention

Talia Zajac, Ottawa
"Truffle Oil"
"1937"
"Runoff"

Guy Simser, Kanata
"Galileo's Nightmare"
"A Shaman's Work"
"A Country Gift"

Cameron R.H. Chown, Arnprior
"It"
"Sister"
"Moment"

Margaret Malloch Zielinski, Ottawa
"Tracking"
"Odyssey"
"Port de Soller"
and also for
"The Dead"
"Emigrant"
"Romantic Relation"

Cyril Dabydeen, Ottawa
"Woman in Water"
"Sitting Cross-Legged in Moonlight"
"Cosmic Dance"

Sylvia Adams, Ottawa
"Guapalo"
"Windows"
"A Word for Time"

Crime/Mystery Poetry

Judged by Fred Kerner, Toronto

1st Place Stewart Boston, Almonte
"Mystery of the Tapestry"
2nd Place Sylvia Adams, Ottawa
"A Letter of Confession"
3rd Place Ruth Latta, Ottawa
"An Old Woman Looks Back"

Short Story

Judged by Bianca Lakoseljac, Toronto

1st Place Suzy Royle, Perth
"Snow"

2nd Place Paul Heffernan, Ottawa
"Hereafter"

3rd Place Helen Gamble, Perth
"All that Jazz"

Honourable Mention

R.L. Brennan, Ottawa
"The Irish Alias"

Barbara Rager, Nepean
"Sanctuary"

Sylvia Adams, Ottawa
"Illusions"

2010

Judged by Victoria Bugdal, Kitchener

1st Place Lawrence Weissmann
"Finding"

"This story absolutely reached through the paper, grabbed me by the shirt collar and wouldn't let me go. I read through a number of stories one night while getting my car serviced at Toyota, and while some I read with interest, this is the only one that night that sucked me in. Everything around me faded away until, of course, I was rudely interrupted by the man who came out to tell me that my car was ready and I was only partially through the story. I raced home and read the rest, hanging on every word. The style was incredible. The flow so easy to follow. The storyline itself resonated with me and I immediately connected with the character, plot and message.

"'Finding' is essentially ageless, as it deals so much with just how we go about our lives — the way we think, feel, and fall victim to our own minds. The moment I read the last word I knew I was holding my winner."

2nd Place Arlene Smith
"Open"

"'Open' challenged me. It was one of the most positively challenging pieces in the mix. I critically looked at each story's plot, structure, style, flow, and grammar. 'Open' was a pleasant read in terms of style and flow. You simply drifted along with each word, sentence, and paragraph with little to no effort. Where it won points with me was the high level of metaphor. Despite what 'Open' means to me, I'm fairly certain that the ultimate meaning is not the same to the next person who reads it, nor the author who wrote it, for that matter. As much as I appreciate a high level of creativity and outside-the-box thinking, 'Open' was the only 'fantasy' story to make it into my top three. I think, in this case, the use of fantasy-based elements was done in such a way that they didn't slap you in the face like most stories do. It seemed real, plausible, and your suspension of disbelief just naturally followed suit."

3rd Place Arlene Smith
"Periods and Pads and Stuff"

"'Periods and Pads and Stuff' was simply entertaining in its Are You There God? It's Me. Margaret kind of way. Then again, perhaps that's a lie, since I haven't read Are You There God? It's Me. Margaret (shameful, I know). I was innocently amused by 'Periods and Pads and Stuff' once again enjoying the story's style and structure. It wasn't until I hit the mid-way point when the perspectives switched that I truly appreciated what the author had created. The plot structure was neat and demonstrated a level of creativity and connectivity not seen in the other stories. 'Periods and Pads and Stuff' ultimately was two stories in one, connected simply by the words in the title, all of which also are homes for multiple meanings. I enjoyed the author's twist on the way we immediately perceive and judge words."

Honourable Mention

Sylvia Braithwaite
"Someday, I'll Take You to Barcelona"

"'Someday, I'll Take You to Barcelona' is one of those heartbreaking stories that you see yourself painfully painted within. You and the character are practically one being and you wonder how the author got into your head and snuck out with all of your thoughts. 'Someday, I'll Take You to Barcelona' describes a place many of us have been, whether we've wanted to be there or not, and in doing so, sucks us into its vortex of familiarity. It's like a warm bowl of comfort food wrapping you up in a literary flurry of cozy pleasure. As much as you know the ending is bittersweet, you know it all too well, and you can't tear yourself away. After all, you've been there yourself and you know that when one door closes, a window elsewhere opens. Not to be cliché, of course."

Gill Foss
"The Luck of the Draw"

"There was something charming about 'The Luck of the Draw' that made me put it aside in my These May Win pile of stories. I enjoyed the initial confusion the story created by the author's unannounced switch between characters. I attempted to figure out, as I went, how they were related and why one character's storyline was so hazy and vague, whereas the other's was much more narrative in nature. Once it becomes clear, you develop an entirely new appreciation for the ways in which both characters, and their stories, have been presented. You see the parallel timeline and appreciate the author's creative and well-styled approach of telling two stories in one."

Carley Centen
"Obituary"

"'Obituary' almost made it into my top three. Heck, it was a mighty contender for my first place. The style, the story telling, the beautiful connection between the main characters and the bittersweet ending made this prose a delight to read. The author has done a fantastic job creating a character with whom we find ourselves empathizing, instead of fearing or loathing, as is described to be the state of individuals within the story. You fall deeper into the folds of their world to see something so much more, only to ultimately be faced with the reality of what we all choose to forget — the fleeting and fading time we have been given."

Poetry

Judged by Bernice Lever, Bowen Island BC

1st Place Sylvia Adams
"Hands, a Choice"

"A poetic essay on three unlikely joined nouns: hands, distance, love, which portray lives through the connective tissue of a miracle: a non-fatal plane crash. A demanding topic, yet magically handled with fresh images that cause the reader to re-examine their own definitions and experiences, especially choices. With wry humour and elegance of diction, this poet creates a reason for sharing love — wherever, whenever it is needed."

2nd Place Margaret Malloch Zielinski
"Blue Willow Plate"

"This poem is a story within a story, unpeeled in layers of just twenty-four unified lines. Enticing the reader through its vivid details 'china so fine whispers pass through' contrasted to 'dog leash dangling from its hook' to a surprising, but necessary conclusion: a new definition of blue caused by horrors. This poet has used an economy of words to develop a memorable message 'Look below the surface.'"

3rd Place Christy Cochrane
"Rain down on the Rideau"

"No spring photograph could be as rewarding as this gentle love poem with artistic metaphors delighting readers with unique images. Yes, there is no rain water, but taste these phrases 'your sticky oar from its fudgey belly', 'a shiver of small peaks', or 'frosting the mixture'. Here, all fifteen lines paint a tableau from a believable fantasy viewpoint."

Honourable Mention

Carol McGrath
"Puberty"

"This extended metaphor encourages readers to re-experience being a young teen bursting with strange sensations. Putting into words the unsettling emotional and physical fluctuations of rapid changes through wild bird comparisons, this poet succeeds in expanding our imaginations."

Adele Graf
"Fog"

"With this poet's words, fog, a common object, becomes a myriad of active energies, moving and creating new interactions and entities for readers. Fresh sensory images please our tongue as fog 'swallows the random footsteps', 'emerges as a plump masseuse', and 'steeps its tea', all flowing in distinctive voice until the last powerful definition. Like all good poems, the reader sees a thing or an event afresh."

Suzanne Nussey
"The Mourner's Bench"

"A strong poem of sorrowing loss is described as the poet's grandfather conducts the service. This poem undulates up and down an emotional range with its parallel of the 'dance of life' in rapid examples of conversion 'from plow to pulpit' and 'foxtrot to God talk' in verse one. Then there's a 'small waxen' newborn in verse two with 'her grief like a small wage'. Ending in steps of yearning love, so like many funerals, people are so tense they don't know whether to laugh or cry or, as this poet writes, 'applaud or pray'. Neither does the reader."

Youth Short Story

Judged by Joan Eyolfson Cadham, Foam Lake Saskatchewan

1st Place Véronique Hynes
"Gushing Pride"

"'Gushing Pride' is the story of a brief encounter told from two points of view. The surprise is that the reader doesn't expect the second viewpoint. We mutter constantly, 'Show, don't tell.' There's nothing 'told' about the two main characters. It is through their reactions and thoughts about the people around them that their personalities are painted in vivid colours. Yes, the clerk obviously does not like old people — but not everyone can tell us so by having him describe one shopper to himself as 'Hunched and ancient, it is Quasimodo with an old lady perm.' The repetition used in this story is the perfect vehicle to carry the personalities and the action."

2nd Place Cassandra Williams
"The Dead Ringer"

"'The Dead Ringer' is a classic horror story, one that does not use artifice or graphic violence. The indescribable horror simply and quietly invades the reader's mind and soul while the bell rings — and rings — and rings. It needs a little line-by-line editing, sometimes just looking for the perfect word. For example, given the era in which the story is placed, Issac would have thought about 'children from the village,' rather than 'kids' — but nothing seriously distracts from the story line. If I have a nightmare tonight, I will be hearing a bell ringing and know I have to go."

3rd Place Véronique Hynes
"Insult Is Injury"

"'Insult Is Injury' is not a typical simplistic story of relationship abuse. The abuse is there, in all its ugliness. However, at the end, the reader is left wondering. Who is the real abuser? Is it he? Or is it she? Or are they caught in a mutual web of their own making? I do not know the age of the author, but this is a thoughtful, mature take on abusive relationships."

Honourable Mention

Samantha Morin
"Hoofbeats"

"Ahhhh. Sigh ... This is a genuine, tender, get-you-where-you-live love story ... even though the lovers are not exactly what we expect in a romance. But it's way more than boy-meets-girl and they race off to happy-ever-after. This richly layered story explores choice, hope, loss, acceptance. Besides, there's one line that, in another context, could describe our own lives in this current North American society 'Races are about returning to the same place over and over, working so hard to get nowhere faster and faster.'"

Breanna Chafe
"Patient X"

"I would say that this story reminds me of O. Henry, except that those foolish kids ('Gift of the Magi') who, in pursuit of frivolous gift-giving, threw away the only possessions they had that were of enduring value, irritate me. 'Patient X', with its own ironic twist, does not. What is real? What is delusion? As the reader, I must confess I was caught completely."

Brittany Graham
"Self Defense"

"This is a short-short that needs no more words. It is chilling. You don't want to think too long about what actually happened. Again, strong characters come alive through conversation and thought. The story is told in the first person and I can't conceive of it working in any other form."

2011

The theme of the 2011 National Capital Writing Contest was "Inspiration Planet Earth Our Natural Environment is Life". Copies of that year's Anthology are available through the branch.

Poetry

1st Place Joan McKay
"And then there was light"

2nd Place Michael Kearsley
"African Dream"

3rd Place, Sylvia Adams
"The Gardener"

Honourable Mention

Ruth Latta
"Chill Mortal"

Carol A. Stephen
"Traffic on Highway 7"

Margaret Malloch Zielinski
"Tracking

Short Story

1st Place Anne Kathleen McLaughlin
"Cairo to Camelot"

2nd Place Gwen Smid
"Sand"

3rd Place Suzy Royle
"Musical Chairs"

Honourable Mention

Colin Morton
"Primavera"

Tudor Robins
"Winter Love"

Fraser White
"Thirst"

Youth Short Story

1st Place Paisley Laurenzio
"Level One"

2nd Place Alison Griffith
"Question Grove"

3rd Place JM (Jennifer) Kempster
"Grey-Washed"

Honourable Mention

Holly Laurenzio
"The Thanksgiving Dinner Disaster"

Christine Molnar
"Breaking the Line"

Christine Molnar
"Going Outside"

2012 Poetry

Judged by Bernice Lever, Bowen Island BC

1st Place Joan McKay
"In the Beginning"

"This poem has the inclusiveness of 'we' as its many visceral words become a magical transport for all our births. Those precise phrases move us quickly to a new magical awareness of our first gasp of air. The poem's pacing emphasizes its unique creation story that echoes in 'a forgotten heartland.' A memorable poem that urges rereading."

2nd Place Maureen Korp
"Friday Afternoon"

"This poet demonstrates the power of contrasting images — in brief or staccato pulses — forcing readers to create their own connections. This poet demands our involvement until we must choose for whom we pray in acts of war, when 'reason flayed' surrounds us."

3rd Place Carol A. Stephen
"Walking in Thompson's Red Sumac"

"A delightful description in accessible, sensory language of a well-loved painter and painting acknowledging once again that fine art is 'alive and well.' Art nourishes us time and time again as it opens our hearts and imaginations as this poem, any piece that 'beckons deeper.'"

Honourable Mention

Alison Griffith
"A Writer's Page"

"Though some poets groan today when hearing rhymes, this poem written with Victorian language does explain our lives. Stressing the pen and 'ivory paper' in this digital world of texting, the poet does depict the problems and prizes of every writer's life. Its fast pacing and exaggerated emotions echo the panic of a waiting white page."

Luminita Suse
"Mammogram"

"This title gives a wealth of meanings radiating from its syllable sounds *ma* and *ma'am* for woman, *mo* for cut or more, and *gram*, so mechanical and measuring against cancer fears, yet also grandma! But the poet's strict, accurate focus draws all into this medical experience, with positive conclusion, 'blooms back into shape.'"

Joan McKay
"In the Middle of this Century (Dust-Covered)"

"This glosa is a poem form in which one poet praises another fine poet by using the theme and style of the quoted poem. This Ottawa-area poet creates the 'back story' in four verses to end each with the four lines of a quoted verse, thus giving them a new life. The poem flows gracefully as the dream's dream explaining the power of longing, until a name recalled can warm our being as it becomes 'more truth than fable.'"

Short Story

Judged by Joan Eyolfson Cadham, Foam Lake, Alberta

1st Place Ken McBeath, Perth
"Walking the Tunnel"

"From the opening sentence, 'The man across from me was about to get a hole in his skull' to the final line, which I will not reveal, this story held me, took me to the setting, introduced me to the characters and insisted I get involved emotionally as quickly as possible and stay that way. No unnecessary descriptions, but I could describe the location of every piece of furniture, because I have seen it."

2nd Place Karen Massey
"Tar Man"

"I don't know whether the author of this piece has a close and intimate knowledge of someone who is intellectually handicapped. Either way, it doesn't matter. This deceptively simple story, told through Zach's point of view, and mostly in Zach's voice, is filled with subtle nuances, quick glimpses into the life of someone whom society perceives as 'different'. It is refreshing, honest, and imaginative."

3rd Place James Hooper
"Shifting Sands"

"Now I know what it's like to walk across a mine field, to know that every step might mean death. I know what drives someone across that field, the reality that, even if you will probably die in the attempt to secure food for your community, you have to get out there and try, anyway. The story, as three young men struggle to reach a misplaced Red Cross food container, makes for compelling reading."

Honourable Mention

Dick Bourgeois-Doyle
"Sylvain et Les Senateurs"

"A Faustian satire about hockey? Oh, yes, it can — and did — happen. Poor Sylvain. Faust bartered his soul to the devil for unlimited knowledge and worldly pleasures. Sylvain just wanted his Ottawa Senators to win the Stanley Cup. It's not easy to write good satire, but this comes close — and the author never loses Sylvain's voice. By the way, your judge is not even a hockey fan."

Roberta Jones
"The Stringhouse"

"A slightly New Age story — but with none of the 'preciousness' and dogma. This is just a good read — and a very carefully crafted one. All the clues are there, although the average reader won't see them until the second read, when they become obvious. And while the main character seems to be trying to convince us that he's really quite curmudgeonly, he most assuredly isn't. Although there are several characters, the author has told the story entirely in the voice of the narrator, with only two lines of other dialogue, and has made it work."

André Narbonne
"My mother is in shadow at the top of the stairs"

"What happens when the kids figure that now they know better than mother does when it comes to deciding where mother should live — or die? This is a current hot topic — the subject of newspaper and magazine articles and radio call-in shows.

"In this short story, the son who has been sent as the Front Guard to convince mother that her days of independent living are over, learns much about himself as he comes to a new understanding about his mother. This story provides a very strong message with no lecturing or preaching, developed skilfully and naturally through the interchanges between mother and son, not an easy task for a writer."

Miriam Sciala
"Music Mag"

"Another hot topic. 'Music Mag' begins with a woman who has been through tough times but is back on her feet and running a successful second-hand shop. But the story is based on Alzheimer's disease, which is about as much as I can say without spoiling the story for future readers or listeners. What happens when you want so very badly to bring back a piece of the past for someone with Alzheimer's? This story is told with great compassion for the attempted giver, the shop owner, and the Alzheimer's victim."

2013

Poetry

Judged by Anne Osborne

1st Place Sylvia Adams, Ottawa
"Old Among Strangers"

2nd Place Karen Massey, Ottawa
"From Industrial Alibis: Angular Momentum"

3rd Place Luminita Suse, Gloucester
"Crows Witness"

Honourable Mention

Jean McKay, Ottawa
"In Beechwood Cemetery"

Gill Foss, Carp
"Undertow (for Gwen)"

Iris Anderson, Ottawa
"Instructions to a Third Grade Teacher"

Youth Short Story

Judged by Noelle Bickle

1st Place Madeline Cuillerier, Ottawa,
Glashan Public School
"A Day in the Life"

"This short story was heartbreaking. The author crafted a story that evoked empathy, compassion, and an in-depth understanding of the inner thoughts of a character consumed by an eating disorder. The biggest strength in this piece was the authentic voice of the narrator — her character was compelling and convincing from the line that read — 'You're on the scale, checking your weight … 120. 90. 110. 100. 90. It settles on 96. Good. That's okay. For now.'

"The level of detail and description written allows the reader to witness the character's desperation and the painstaking efforts she makes with this disorder. The reader is simply compelled to read on. There are small details hidden like gems in this piece as well. 'It sounds exactly like when you pour your medicine down the drain.' There is much revealed in this line, yet in a controlled manner — letting the reader receive crucial information in a way that is skilful and understated. The reader knows there is more story behind that sentence, but we don't need to be led there with drawn-out explanations. The author has delivered the message with simplicity — we get it. Well done. This poignant story, one filled with depth in terms of story and narrative voice, is very deserving of first place in the competition."

2nd Place Patrick Gloutney
"Sudden Impact"

"The author of 'Sudden Impact' clearly has in-depth knowledge of the dynamics of flight, as per the level of detail and description in this short story. There are interesting elements incorporated into the story that depict the simulation of war and the tension and chaos that comes in that moment. The author did an excellent job of building tension during that crash scene — it had this reader on the edge of my seat. The dialogue flowed very well — not an easy task during such a tense scene — but the dialogue throughout was well paced and rang true. The author did a great job at developing a fast-paced story with great tension and dialogue."

3rd Place Alison Griffith
"The Story of Them"

"The author paints a picture of a seemingly perfect world, with a distorted and impossible relationship at the very core of it. The reader can feel the main character's isolation and heartbreak. Throughout this piece is interesting language 'granted, the man had never cared a fig for convention' — which takes us to a different time and place. Another strength to this piece is the beautiful phrase depicting the character's pain and sorrow, 'eyes shadowed by a rich shade of purple that would have been beautiful anywhere else', and 'it fuelled her resilience, preventing the inevitable cut from growing too deep. 'The Story of Them' is a tangled and emotional story that reads like a classic tale of a young woman's despair and isolation.

2014

Judged by: Rose-Ann Marchitto, Barrie, Ontario

Short Story

1st Place Arlene Smith, Nepean
"Life Expos-ed"

"'Hot dog buns make excellent pillows.' What a great opening line. I immediately wanted to read more. The author's skill of weaving a story stood out as even though we knew the ending, it was exciting to keep turning pages and find out how the day at Shea Stadium developed. Each of the characters was fully developed, I felt like I knew them."

2nd Place Anne C. Rumin, Ottawa
"Misha"

"The story of Misha is extremely sad but realistic. The love for this child, the loneliness of taking care of him, the paranoia of what would happen when the caretaker dies, are all felt on the page. It's a story that sparks empathy and controversy at the same time. Beautifully done."

3rd Place Corey Reed, Vanier
"Miles To Go"

"A sad story but well developed. I could feel his angst and hoped like he did that Miles would arrive. I liked the sensory detail, the deep groove in his reliable old lazy chair. When Allen ran out to see who was coming, convinced it was his friend Miles, I wanted to scream after him, and yell no-way. The end left me wondering."

Honourable Mention

Christine Beelen, Ottawa
"Market Girl"

"An interesting read that shows development. As Sue sorts through the details of a new life, a new apartment and the aloneness of being an empty nester, she finds hope in the ability to help someone else. This story is full of a promise of healing and goodness."

Bruce MacGregor, Ottawa
"The Date"

"Skilfully told. The interweaving of details so we learn of the dismantling of Colleen's old life and the glimpse into what could be her future is well done."

Sonia Qin, Ottawa
"The Contract Dream"

"What I liked about this story is the concept. While a good story on its own, this could have a potential to be more. The dystopian feel would work well as a book. The characters are well thought out. I cared from the first page."

Poetry

Judged by Keith Inman, Thorold, Ontario

1st Place Catina Noble, Ottawa
"You Can't See Me"

"Depth of clarity without fluff; the right amount of information for the reader to know what is going on; the story of this poem is sparse, bare and direct. Line breaks are well handled to the point that they do not necessarily end on hard, strong counts. Weakness is shown, 'because', 'of'. And the hanging, unwritten question at the end, is he really gone for good? Well, in the instant of the poem, of the emotion shown, there is hope. We see this person."

2nd Place Joan McKay, Ottawa
"I Love you as Certain Dark Things are Loved"

"Using quotes from another poem (cento poetry) is a great exercise. This poem does that extremely well. The transitions between writer's lines and the quotes are seamless, which is hard to achieve when using this style. And the way the author captures the essence of the original quote in lines like, 'But I don't love you for what is Strauss or Jazz' is excellent."

3rd Place Helen Gamble
"Listen"

"The sheer simplicity of this poem is astounding. Even though it doesn't use sound, it does use metaphors of silence to describe a lack of sound that makes you think of sound, makes you want to listen. Enough said."

Honourable Mention

Sylvia Adams
"The Importance of Preserving Blue"

"This poem stood out from the beginning as something special. The opening line, a statement, begs the question, How to write without blue? Then it shows you. The tone is consistent. The matter put before us, 'No clothesline Banter.' And later, the challenge, 'do you remember,' keeps the reader engaged."

Karen Massey
"Cool House, or Sestina for the Time Being"

"The brilliance, here, is everyday language, 'Oh, don't bother with that, let's walk.' That usage, along with varied and enjambed lines, hides the set pattern. Best example, Philip Larkin's, 'Whitsun Wedding'. In 'Cool House, or Sestina for the Time Being', the love/labour is a smooth mix of rant, rap and story telling rhyme, 'stink trouble, fierce trouble, worst kind of trouble.'"

Patricia Kirby
"Grateful for Strangers"

"The poem starts in the present and works back through 'lost meanings' to claim 'When you live for several centuries/on a spit of sand.' An impossible life span. But this poem is about isolation and people. The 'you' is not singular. It's a history of people, leaving their mark, so beautifully told in the last three lines."

2015

Poetry

1st Place Karen Massey
"in sequins, dulling"

2nd Place Carol McGrath
"Sky Maps"

3rd Place Joan McKay
"Winter Blues"

Honourable Mention

Gerry Mooney (Ms)
"A Sky Suite"

Gill Foss
"The Art of Discovery"

Joan McKay
"Stardust"

Short Story

1st Place Anna C Rumin
"Ned and Lill"

2nd Place Cynthia Clegg
"The Reception"

3rd Place James Palmer
"Birthday"

Honourable Mention

Jennifer Hanlon-Wilde
"This Space Intentionally Left Blank"

Zenon Strzelczyk
"The Inward Vision"

Stephanie Loiza Read
"Tara Marie Andronek"

2016 Poetry

Judged by Sheila Martindale, Victoria, British Columbia

1st Place Gill Foss
"Green Shift"

"This poem works on many different levels: celebrating the end of winter, and describing the coming of spring with a lovely economy of words. There is a lyricism here which lulls the reader into believing this is a pastoral poem — until the last stanza and the right hook of an environmental message. Beautiful!"

2nd Place Sylvia Adams
"High School Reunion"

"This poem packs a punch! High school reunions are bittersweet, and the poet has caught the spirit of the thing — how everything looks so small, how there is no sign of those who disgraced themselves by getting pregnant or who were caught stealing, and how the line of chairs by the wall is reminiscent of former wallflowers at the school dance. A great poem full of atmosphere!"

3rd Place Helen Gamble
"Feeding the Flowers"

"A wonderfully evocative poem about an elderly caretaker in an old cemetery. In a few short stanzas, the poet has given us a picture of the man, the work he did, his dedication. And now that he is gone … This poem touches the heart without being in the least bit sentimental."

Honourary Mention

Lee Ann Eckhardt Smith
"Christmas Baking"

Gerry Mooney
"A Piece of Scotch Plaid"

Gerry Mooney
"Preparing for Winter"

Short Story

Judged by Matthew Bin, Oakville, Ontario

1st Place Lynn Jatania
"What the Chipmunk is Thinking"

"A truly well-told tale of three characters in three different lonely situations. The author engages with these characters with empathy and humour, without straying into cloying sentimentality. The result is a story that is not easy, but is immensely satisfying."

2nd Place Tony Bove
"The Step-Mother's Story: We Never Called Her Cinderella"

"A fairy tale retelling that is not for children, or indeed for the faint of heart. Considering the Cinderella story from her step-family's point of view is eye-widening and discomfiting, and this story stays with the reader for long afterwards."

Third Place Adrienne Stevenson
"Leveller"

"The prose is as sparse and unforgiving as the landscape in this post-apocalyptic setting. The sharp, raw story is short but unrelenting, and the conclusion is satisfyingly disturbing."

Honourable Mention

Arlene Somerton-Smith
"A Stone in the Temple"

Josephine Bolechala
"Mask Island"

Adam Heenan
"Benny and Margot Forever"

The Graphics Artist

Catina Noble is a mixed media artist and author. In 2014, her poem "You Can't See Me" won 1st Place in the NCWC's Poetry Division.

In fall 2015, her art work was featured in Ottawa's Chinatown Remixed Festival. She is currently working on illustrations for an upcoming poetry anthology *Transitory Tango* due out August 2017. Catina teaches a children's art class at the Dempsey Community Centre in Ottawa.

She is the author of *Katzenjammer*; *I'm Glad I Didn't Kill Myself* (Reader's Favourite); and *Vacancy at the Food Court & Other Short Stories*. Her next book, *Lost at 13*, is due out May 2017.

The NCWC Coordinator/Anthology Designer

Except for 2014, Sherrill Wark has handled the entries for the NCWC since its 22nd year, 2009.

"It's not a job for the faint of heart," she says, "but growing up in Renfrew, Ontario, with the Chief of Police as a father makes 'Rules are Rules' part of my psyche." She laughs. "Although, having a cop for a father also makes 'Rules are there for the breaking' part of my psyche, too. Cops' kids and ministers' kids, eh?"

"Most entrants are extremely diligent so it's only rarely I have to toss an entry. And I do this always with a certain amount of sadness. By the way, I can't count the number of entries with tape on the flap of the envelope. I find this endearing as I've done it many a time, too. Either to ensure the contents are safe, or to double-check that everything's been included." To lighten things up, she refers to herself as the BATG (the Bitch At The Gate). Sherrill is a former dog breeder/dog show enthusiast so uses the word "bitch" with no connotations other than "bitches are our mommy dogs therefore a reputable breeder's most precious commodity." Please note in the photo that there is no actual fence, only a gate.

Occasionally, Sherrill will get an e-mail from an entrant, "OMG, I forgot to put my cheque in! May I send it to you?" If this happens prior to the closing date, there would be no issues arise from her agreeing to this. On the other hand, this year, Sherrill received an e-mail from a potential entrant a week after the closing date asking if there might be leeway, could he still send in his entry anyway. Her response was along the lines of "With deepest regret ..."

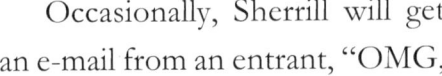
The BATG.

Sherrill enjoys the fever surrounding the NCWC. As the entries start trickling in there's always the fear that this year things will be slow, but the mountain of entries that arrives just before closing date reassures her that Canada's writing community is alive and well and still competitive. (Prior to 2017, the contest was open only to writers in the Ottawa area. It is now open across Canada.) Awards Night is electric with anticipation and excitement.

Sherrill Wark is the author of *Mostly of Love & the Perils Thereof: The Sequel*; *The Closet Hides a Flight of Stairs* (both poetry); *Really Stupid Writing Mistakes: How to Avoid Them* (non-fiction); *Death in l'Acadie: a Kesk8a story*; *Refuge in l'Acadie: a Kesk8a story* (both historical fiction, the first two of a planned six in the series about the Acadians from the viewpoint of a Mi'qmaw woman); and most recently, *Graven Images* (horror). She also writes screenplays, one of which, *The Bus to*

Lo Siento, made it into the top 10% of the 2013 Oaxaca Film Fest. Sherrill has also written under the pseudonym Christina Crowe: *My Search for Serotonin: Experiences of Suicidal Depression and How to Deal with It* (a blog turned into a book, and now a free e-book at Smashwords: https://www.smashwords.com/); *A Girl Dog's Breakfast: Scary Stories and Rude Poems*; and *The Unkindest Cut: Short Creepy Movie Scripts*.

Made in the USA
Middletown, DE
03 June 2017